The Women's Concise Guide
to Emotional Well-Being

THE WOMEN'S
CONCISE GUIDE TO
EMOTIONAL
WELL-BEING

Karen J. Carlson, M.D.

Stephanie A. Eisenstat, M.D.

Terra Ziporyn, Ph.D.

Harvard University Press
Cambridge, Massachusetts
London, England • 1997

Library of Congress Cataloging-in-Publication Data

Carlson, Karen J.
The women's concise guide to emotional well-being / Karen J.
Carlson, Stephanie A. Eisenstat, Terra Ziporyn.
p.   cm.
Includes bibliographical references and index.
ISBN 0-674-95490-4 (cloth). — ISBN 0-674-95491-2 (paper)
1. Women–Mental health. I. Eisenstat, Stephanie A.
II. Ziporyn, Terra Diane, 1958–   . III. Title.
RC451.4.W6C37   1997
616.89′0082–dc21   97-21277

Contents

Violence and Mental Health

Sexual Behavior of Women

Taking Control

Seeking Help

The Women's Concise Guide
to Emotional Well-Being

Introduction

Mainstream medicine increasingly recognizes—or, more accurately, remembers—that health and well-being are complex products of body, mind, and environment. Women in particular have been acutely aware of these interrelationships, long before formal scientific studies began validating them. Across time and cultures, women have discovered that fear or stress can delay a menstrual period, that lifestyle changes can diminish sex drive, that deep breathing and a supportive partner can help relieve the pain of childbirth.

Today, clinicians who specialize in women's health routinely ask patients not just about aches and pains but also about family worries, work habits, sexual concerns, and sleep problems. Their attention to the whole patient rather than just a diseased body part is prompted by accumulating evidence from the relatively new field of psychoneuroimmunology, which explores the way behavior and emotions influence the nervous and immune systems. Findings from this field are beginning to confirm what healers have maintained from earliest times: healing the mind is integral to healing the body, and vice versa. It is increasingly clear that emotional and social health—solid coping skills, a sense of control over one's life, connections with other people, adequate food and shelter, freedom from fear of violence, and an underlying sense of hope—all go hand-in-hand with physical health.

Although evidence so far has not convinced medical scientists that improving one's mental state can actually cure or prevent diseases, the new findings do open possibilities for easing the discomfort of disease, surgery, or chemotherapy. More and more mainstream clinicians are using certain mind-body techniques (usually in combination with conventional drugs or surgery) to treat problems ranging from anxiety, depression, and phobias to premenstrual syndrome, eating disorders, and chronic pain. There is even some evidence that joining a support group may improve survival rates among women with breast cancer. Some researchers think that perhaps the enhanced social support from other members of the group improves the immune system's ability to combat cancer cells. Among the most promising mind-body techniques being investigated and used today are biofeedback, hypnosis, relaxation exercises, assertiveness training, cognitive therapy, meditation, yoga, deep breathing, and various forms of stress management.

While disorders of the mind can have physical consequences, and disorders of the body can lead to emotional disturbance, often we cannot neatly separate cause from effect. For example, we know that women who have a poor body image are more susceptible to anorexia nervosa, but we also know that this eating disorder disturbs a woman's neurochemistry, leading her to see herself as intolerably obese while objective observers see her as emaciated. During menopause, a woman may feel depressed because her youth has passed, but if hot flashes and drenching sweats are disrupting her sleep night after night, it is not easy to know if her depression originates in cultural stereotypes or in chronic sleep deprivation—or a combination of the two.

Similarly, substance abuse in women may stem from social and economic distress, emotional disorders, or physical illness, but once an addiction develops, it will have repercussions in all these other areas of life, making the roots of the problem difficult to disentangle. Childhood sexual or physical abuse not only leaves emotional scars but also makes women unusually susceptible to seemingly unrelated physical ailments in adulthood—irritable bowel syndrome, backaches, shortness of breath, abdominal and pelvic pain. Women subjected to domestic abuse often complain of physical disorders that cannot be traced directly to injuries, such as headaches, insomnia, and fatigue; and they may try to hide, or be unaware of, psychological disorders in themselves that are caused by living in a state of constant fear and hopelessness.

Differences between the sexes. Women are twice as likely as men to have panic attacks, 4 times as likely to have seasonal affective disorder (SAD), and 9 times as likely to have an eating disorder.

One woman out of every 3 becomes clinically depressed during her lifetime, in contrast with about 1 man in 9. Women are also 2 to 4 times more likely than men to have been sexually abused as children; in fact, recent studies indicate that 1 out of every 4 adult women has been involved in a nonvoluntary sexual encounter before the age of 18.

Although women and men frequently receive the same psychiatric diagnosis, the causes of a given condition in the two sexes are often radically different, as are the effects. For example, posttraumatic stress disorder in women is more likely to result from rape, incest, and domestic abuse than from military combat or torture, the common causes in men. And while men with a history of trauma tend to direct their anger outward in acts of aggression or violence, women who have a history of trauma commonly withdraw, becoming depressed or alcoholic. Male substance abusers are more likely to have legal and job-related problems, whereas women who abuse drugs or alcohol are prone to develop family and marital problems. These women are also more likely than their male counterparts to have a psychiatric illness such as depression, and after seeking treatment they end up divorced much more frequently than do men.

In the not-so-distant past, the cultural stereotype of women as overly emotional and irrational led physicians to label physical disorders in women (particularly disorders that were difficult to diagnose) as symptoms of hysteria or hypochondria. Even today, some women who are eventually diagnosed as having fibromyalgia, chronic fatigue syndrome, interstitial cystitis, endometriosis, postpartum depression, or premenstrual syndrome spend several frustrating years being told by friends and professionals alike that their symptoms are all in their heads.

The nineteenth-century diagnosis of hysteria is no longer made, but feminist psychiatrists believe that certain modern diagnostic categories continue to stigmatize women, labeling as mental illnesses behaviors that are essentially coping styles. Among these suspect diagnostic categories are borderline personality disorder, histrionic personality disorder, multiple personality disorder, and somatization disorder, to name just a few. These diagnoses are made predominantly in women, and, according to some feminist critics, all of them would be better understood as variants on posttraumatic stress disorder. Indeed, a high percentage of women who receive these diagnoses have been physically or sexually abused.

Even in the case of depression, feminist psychotherapists emphasize the cultural rather than biological differences between men and women that may account for different incidences of this disease. They point out that in a society which elevates self-sufficiency above other interpersonal qualities, the tendency of women to value intimacy over independence becomes a weakness, leading to loss of self-esteem and, in many cases, depression. More mainstream investigators agree that depression in women has a cultural component, but they see the disorder as a constellation of sociocultural, biological, and economic factors that in our society hit women harder than men. These include marital discord, the stress of balancing a job with childcare, living in poverty (particularly in an urban environment), being a member of a stigmatized group (minority, lesbian, or overweight, for example), being discriminated against, sexually harassed, or underpaid in the workplace, and having a history of sexual or physical abuse.

Women and stress. Many of the differences between men and women's emotional health may be linked to the different kinds of stress they experience—and the way they react to them. The physiological stress response (also known as the fight-or-flight response) seems to be triggered by different situations in women than in men, and to have different physical effects. In general, while men find competition and intellectual challenge particularly stressful, interpersonal conflict is more stressful to most women. Feelings of anger and impatience seem to increase the risk of heart attack in men, whereas suppressing anger—a behavior much more common in women—seems to raise the risk of developing high blood pressure, obesity, headaches, and depression.

A recent report by the U.S. Department of Labor revealed that working women rank stress as their greatest everyday problem. Most of the complaints came from women in their 40s who had professional and managerial jobs, as well as from single mothers who said that their biggest problem is balancing family and work and finding affordable childcare. Adding to women's stress were concerns about pay (which is still on average only 71 percent of that of men with comparable training and responsibilities) and the lack of adequate health insurance.

Whatever its source, prolonged stress in any woman can make her more susceptible to reproductive problems, premenstrual syndrome, headaches, sleep disorders, back pain, gastrointestinal woes, and a wide range of emotional disorders. As more studies get under way, other conditions particularly common among women may be added to the list of stress-induced illnesses: lupus, multiple sclerosis, rheumatoid arthritis, and other autoimmune diseases. Conversely, physical disease, whether in a woman herself or in family members under her care, frequently adds a huge burden of stress to the ordinary tensions of daily life.

Hiding behind the physical. With all the emphasis on the new fields of women's primary care, behavioral medicine, and alternative therapies, it may come as a surprise that emotional disturbance and mental illness in women still often go undetected by primary care clinicians. Some kinds of questions on the minds of women patients may not be addressed during a busy office visit, including questions concerning bouts of anxiety, symptoms of depression, postpartum psychiatric disorders, sleep disturbance, and drinking habits. Other concerns may not be clearly articulated, often out of a sense of privacy, embarrassment, or perhaps even denial—worries about domestic violence, sexual preference, sexual response, and substance abuse. For instance, a woman may seek help for migraine headaches, but never mention that she is also having trouble sleeping or that she feels overwhelmed by a sense of despair. Similarly, a woman may consult a specialist about constant fatigue, without bringing up her child's chronic illness or her eighty-hour work week. Another woman may complain of irritable bowel syndrome, without realizing that the sexual abuse she suffered as a child may be relevant to her physical symptoms.

This book attempts to raise some of these questions about the psychological and social factors that so often influence a woman's well-being. Recognizing the complex interplay of body, mind, and culture, we have attempted to cover a wide variety of subjects in the area of women's mental and emotional health, and to offer ways in which women from all walks of life can better manage stress and the other psychological challenges they face. These include using relaxation techniques such as meditation and hypnosis; finding reliable sources of social support; learning to confront anger and express negative emotions effectively; rechanneling responses to underlying thoughts and feelings; and adopting a healthier lifestyle by improving eating and exercise habits, losing weight, cutting out cigarettes, and getting enough sleep. There are also guidelines to help women assess when professional counseling may be indicated.

The psychological and emotional aspects of subjects unique to women, such as postpartum depression, premenstrual syndrome, and menopause, are discussed, as well as mental health problems of special concern to younger women and to elderly women or their caretakers (anorexia and Alzheimer's disease are two examples). Because certain emotional issues change dramatically over the life span, topics such as body image and depression are organized around the changing circumstances of women as they age.

By highlighting what we currently know about the mental and psychological disturbances that afflict women—their causes and their cures—we hope to help women everywhere become informed partners with their clinicians as they work toward the common goal of good health and emotional well-being.

Depression

Depression in Women

Depression encompasses a wide variety of emotional and mental states, ranging from sadness and low self-esteem to disabling apathy and suicidal behavior. It may develop in reaction to some outside event, such as the death of a loved one, or it may have no apparent cause. The former is called reactive depression and the latter clinical depression.

Psychiatrists further divide depression into types depending primarily on the severity and nature of symptoms. In women the most prevalent types of depression are dysthymia (once called depressive neurosis) and major depression. Dysthymia usually begins during childhood or adolescence and is characterized by sadness, negative attitude, and low self-esteem. Major depression involves similar but much more severe, sometimes intolerable symptoms. It usually begins in the late 20s but may occur at any time. A related mood disorder is manic-depressive disorder (see below), which is marked by cycles of mania and depression.

At the molecular level depression is thought to be caused by inadequate amounts of neurotransmitters in the brain. This disturbance can result from numerous physical illnesses, as well as reactions to certain medications, including beta blockers, diet pills, tranquilizers, oral contraceptives, and alcohol. Some people are particularly vulnerable to depression for genetic reasons; the disorder is more likely to occur in people whose parents or siblings have a history of depression.

But there are other risk factors for depression that do not readily lend themselves to a biological explanation: a history of sexual or physical abuse, marital discord, or having children under the age of 5 at home, as well as living in poverty or in an urban environment, to name a few. In a given individual the ultimate explanation for depression may be a constellation of interrelated factors—sociocultural as well as biological. Being a member of a stigmatized group (a minority or a lesbian, for example) may increase a woman's risk for depression.

▸ What are the symptoms?

Everybody is sad or blue now and then because of job loss, death of a loved one, a failed romance, and the like. Clinical depression occurs when this sadness lasts longer than it should or when it is intense enough to interfere with normal functioning. Depressed people feel persistent numbness, helplessness, hopelessness, worthlessness, and guilt. They generally lose interest in life, work, and other activities they previously found pleasurable, including sex. Life may feel so gloomy or meaningless that suicide seems the only solution—and sometimes it is attempted. For others, particularly adolescents, the apparent solution may come in the form of alcohol and substance abuse, which can lead to further depression.

Many people with depression have trouble thinking, concentrating, remembering, responding, and making decisions, and some experience hallucinations or delusions, as well as anxiety and psychosomatic disorders. They also commonly have physical symptoms such as appetite changes, weight loss or gain, dizziness, headaches, inexplicable weeping or sad facial expressions, sleeping too much or sleeping too little (insomnia), early morning awakening, and fatigue. Depression frequently coexists with hostility. This can be directed toward the source of the problematic relationship (such as the spouse) or deflected toward others (such as the children).

▸ Who is likely to develop depression?

Depression appears at least twice as often in American women as in American men. It afflicts at least 1 woman in 10 at any given time; and as many as 1 woman in 3 may become clinically depressed at some point during her lifetime, in contrast to about 1 man in 9.

Why women are so prone to depression is the subject of many theories and much active investigation. Some feminist psychologists believe that the interpersonal and relationship issues may be more relevant than the biological ones in understanding women's depression. Proponents of this "psychosocial" approach regard depression as a reaction to certain stressful developments throughout the life span—mainly involving women's relationships to work, family, and health changes.

According to this view, women tend to interpret the world in terms of personal relationships, whereas men rely more on abstract laws and rules. From an early age women generally seek to cultivate and maintain their connections with others, but their lifelong quest for intimacy is viewed as a weakness in a culture that values self-sufficiency and independence. The discrepancy between the behavior of most women and the values of the culture leads to a loss of self-esteem, a feeling of "just not being good enough."

Moreover, because of a power imbalance between the sexes, this argument goes, it is hard for a woman to establish and maintain connections with others while preserving her inner or "true" self. In many women the inner self is "silenced" for the sake of preserving relationships. Often physical or emotional abuse forces this silence on women, but many women also end up silencing themselves. The high price they pay for "saving" their relationships in this way is depression.

Depression may occur because women feel they cannot be themselves in their relationships and must conform to someone else's idea of what a good woman, partner, or mother should be. Even when they accept the standard, many women become depressed when they discover that they are simply unable to live up to it. Throughout the life span, according to this theory, the priority that women give to maintaining personal connections can lead to stresses that precipitate depression. Whether they work inside or outside the home, whether they choose to have children or not, whether they choose men or other women as partners, women still find that their relationships are the primary source of both meaning in their lives and depression.

Depression in premenopausal women. Major depression is most common in women between 18 and 44, with the late 20s being the average age at which it begins. For those who marry in their early 20s, marital discord often peaks at about this time (roughly 7 years into a marriage), and unhappily married women (as well as lesbians in unhappy relationships) show more clinical depression than unmarried women or women who are satisfied with their partners. Having and caring for young children, also common in this age group, only increases the risk of depression. Many studies suggest that couples with young children feel more stress and pressure than any other family group. Research also shows that in cultures where there is greater access to childcare and support for childrearing, rates of depression in women are lower.

One of the possible connections between depression, marriage, and children may be that women feel overwhelmed by, and often experience conflict over, family responsibility. Even as more husbands take on additional obligations in the home, women continue to bear the biggest burden of time and emotional strain for childcare and housework. Juggling long commutes, inadequate childcare, unequal domestic responsibilities, sleep deprivation, care for sick children, homework, and a full-time job can drain life of joy and turn it into little more than a series of self-denying duties.

Despite all these stresses on the working mother, there is a slightly greater risk of depression in women who are at home full-time with young children. This is probably because working women have greater access to social support, and work provides an alternative source of pride, gratification, and self-esteem. Housework is a notoriously lonely and cyclic activity which brings little external reward. Mothers do not get a raise for keeping cupboards neat or getting up at 3 A.M. to coerce a screaming toddler into swallowing a dropperful of medicine. For many women the self-sacrifice and tiring, repetitious tasks of childcare dilute its intrinsic challenges and rewards.

Infertility problems in their late 20s and 30s start many women down the road to depression. Attempts to conceive a child often involve costly and invasive medical procedures, and the uncertainty, or failure, associated with infertility can shake the foundations of a couple's relationship—especially if the woman feels the stigma of infertility more strongly than her partner or if either partner raises issues of guilt or blame. Conceiving and rearing children can be especially stressful issues for lesbian women (see Sexual Preference).

Divorce, though it affects every age group, is particularly likely tounderlie depression in premenopausal women. Divorce is most likely to occur during the early years of a marriage, in childless marriages, among those who marry young, and among people who come from families with unhappy marriages. To a woman in her late

20s or 30s who has children, divorce may raise the specter of poverty and economic hardship, as well as fears for the welfare of her children. To a woman in a childless marriage, divorce may seem to slam the door on the possibility of ever having a family of her own.

Depression in the 40s and 50s. Many women who become depressed at menopause have suffered from depression previously or have other life problems that can account for the depression. Menopause itself does not increase a woman's risk for depression, but women who have many physical symptoms at menopause do experience more transient depressive symptoms than those who go through menopause with hardly a hot flash or sleepless night.

What is more common in women in their 40s and 50s is a mild melancholy over impending health changes. For the first time in their lives women may find themselves dealing with high blood pressure or struggling with unwanted weight gain. Menopausal symptoms, sometimes troubling in themselves, may be a reminder of these other changes. The physical symptoms of menopause seem to be worse in women with depression and in women who did not know what to expect from menopause. Menopause may also intensify feelings of loss among both heterosexual and lesbian women who were unable to conceive children, or who chose not to have children earlier in their life.

Women in their 40s and 50s are more likely to have teenage children. Intense emotional outbursts from adolescents are upsetting and can lead to discord between parents. Divorce in this age group is often precipitated by extramarital affairs, which can be particularly threatening to a woman who is no longer young. Depression at this time of life (in either sex) may relate to facing mortality and the finitude of life. A woman in particular may dwell on the failing health of her husband and the possibility of being widowed. Also during these decades many women take on the care of elderly parents, or are forced to place them in a nursing home. The stress, guilt, and grief that come from attending the slow death of a mother or father leaves many middle-aged women depressed.

Depression in the elderly. Risk factors in this age group include stress, losses, maladaptive personality styles, and previous histories of psychiatric or physical illness. Depression is the most common psychological problem among older women.

Often older women are diagnosed for depression only when they are seen by a doctor for some other reason, usually a physical ailment. At times the depression itself may result in some physical problem without the woman's ever realizing that she is depressed (see Psychosomatic Disorders). Too often some of the mental symptoms of depression are mistaken for signs of senility or Alzheimer's disease.

By contrast, some women are treated for mild depression unnecessarily. One study found that although people between 60 and 74 had fewer life crises and less psychic distress than any other age group, they were more likely to be prescribed psychoactive medications. Forty-four percent of the women in this study had received a prescription for such a drug in the previous year, and 20 percent were taking these medications on a regular basis. This overmedication may be related to the fact that older people visit physicians more often than younger ones. Whatever the cause, it remains a concern because psychoactive drugs tend to have a higher rate of adverse effects in the elderly.

▸ How is the condition evaluated?
Because patients often mask depression with a physical complaint, doctors can easily overlook it. Many people suffering from depression try to downplay their emotional symptoms, and even if a doctor does diagnose depression, many patients have trouble accepting it.

Primary care providers who suspect depression use various tests and questions to evaluate it and distinguish major depression from dysthymia and other forms. Part of the evaluation involves determining if the patient has any underlying medical conditions or is taking any medications known to cause depression.

In addition, the primary care provider will want to determine if there is any risk of suicide. These findings will be taken very seriously. Any patient contemplating suicide will be sent for evaluation and treatment by a mental health professional, who will then decide whether hospitalization is necessary. Patients with depression who are abusing drugs or alcohol or who have symptoms of psychosis (such as hallucinations), a history of failed treatments, or severe symptoms will also be referred to a psychotherapist for further evaluation and treatment.

▸ How is depression treated?

Depression is usually treated with some combination of psychotherapy and antidepressant medications. Short-term psychotherapy is particularly effective in treating reactive depression in women who have marital, family, or work-related stresses. It is also recommended for women with mild depression or dysthymia and for those who choose not to take medication.

Cognitive therapy (which can be short-term or longer) can help a patient change negative patterns of thinking, while other forms of behavior therapy (including assertiveness training) can help a patient change inappropriate behaviors.

Many women with depression can benefit from either family or marital counseling. A psychotherapist sensitive to women's issues can help the patient find ways to develop healthy, mature forms of interdependence that are free from compulsive caretaking and repression of the self.

Antidepressants (see below)—drugs that elevate mood— are often prescribed in conjunction with psychotherapy and are effective in about 65 percent of people with depression. They are most appropriately used for patients with a family history of depression, who have had 3 or more previous episodes of depression, or who have severe symptoms.

Many psychotherapists emphasize that individuals with depression cannot be healed in isolation. Because the self is shaped by its relationships with others, it can only be reshaped through those relationships. Again and again, social support (which many depressed people shun) has been shown to be a buffer against depression.

Antidepressants

In the past, the most commonly used drugs in treating depression were the tricyclic antidepressants (TCAs) imipramine (Tofranil) and amitriptyline (Elavil), or, when these failed, the monoamine oxidase inhibitors (MAOIs) phenelzine (Nardil) and tranylcypromine sulfate (Parnate). These drugs often have disturbing side effects, including dry mouth, drowsiness, lightheadedness, and weight gain, and cannot be used by people with a variety of other medical conditions.

▸ Selective serotonin reuptake inhibitors (SSRIs)

In the recent past, tricyclic antidepressants and MAOIs have largely been replaced by Prozac (fluoxetine), a drug that has become almost a household word (much as Valium was in the 1960s). Prozac, as well as the related drugs Zoloft (sertraline) and Paxil (paroxetine), works by selectively raising levels in the brain of serotonin, the neurotransmitter thought to be most responsible for regulating moods. Because of its specificity, Prozac has far fewer side effects than TCAs and MAOIs, and it is safe for use during pregnancy. Some 5 million Americans have taken Prozac, and over 900,000 prescriptions for it are written every month.

All of this has led some observers to worry about the ethical implications of the growing reliance on "magic pills" such as Prozac to treat not only major depression but chronic low-level depression as well. This tendency will undoubtedly be exacerbated in the future by attempts at health care cost-cutting, since prescription drugs are cheaper than long-term psychotherapy.

Critics of this trend worry about the still unknown health and social impact of what they call "cosmetic psychopharmacology." They suggest that by medicalizing unhappiness, we may be altering the human personality as well as relieving depression. Proponents of Prozac counter that there is nothing wrong with making the human condition happier if it can be done so easily. Others add that Prozac's ability to transform human personality is poorly documented; they suggest that such drastic changes may occur in only a small number of people who use the drug, hardly enough to justify these weighty ethical questions.

Indeed, some people with mild depression are disappointed when they try Prozac or one of its relatives. Although these drugs often improve mood, many women report that they cause difficulty having orgasms. A number of women with mild depression who stop using the drugs give this as their major reason.

▸ Alternative antidepressants

To determine the appropriate antidepressant, a woman and her doctor must discuss her individual symptoms of depression, cost considerations, and potential side effects of treatment. Knowing, for example, that Prozac tends to promote weight loss while TCAs tend to cause weight gain may make a difference to many women. Similarly, a woman whose depression involves severe insomnia may do best with a TCA taken at bedtime because these drugs often act as sedatives. And despite the common side effects, a woman whose depression is unrelieved by other antidepressants may benefit from MAOIs taken under the supervision of a psychiatrist.

A woman with both anxiety and depression who is taking antianxiety drugs such as alprazolam (Xanax) should talk with her doctor about switching to an antidepressant. Antianxiety drugs are ineffective in treating depression, and, unlike antidepressants, they can be addictive. Much of the time taking antidepressants alone will alleviate any associated anxiety.

Whatever antidepressant is eventually prescribed, women should schedule a physician visit within one month after starting treatment so that side effects can be monitored and dosages adjusted accordingly. After that, most women will continue to see their doctor periodically. The decision about when to stop therapy can usually be made jointly by the woman and her doctor.

After a single incident of major depression, it is often possible to stop medications gradually after 6 to 12 months, resuming treatment if symptoms recur. Some doctors feel that long-term medication may be more appropriate for patients who have a history of recurrence, a family history of manic depression, onset of symptoms before age 20, or severe, sudden, or life-threatening symptoms.

Seasonal Affective Disorder

Seasonal affective disorder is a recurrent form of depression which develops during the fall and winter months and disappears during the spring and summer. Much more severe than the "winter blahs" or the "holiday blues," SAD makes people go into a sort of hibernation during the dark and dreary months, which involves long periods of sleep, withdrawal from the world, and stocking up on high-calorie sweets and carbohydrates.

In the past decade psychiatrists and other members of the medical community have come to recognize SAD as a legitimate diagnostic category. Some investigators estimate that as many as 10 million Americans suffer from this disorder, and as many as 25 million—or 1 in 5 Americans—may suffer from a mild form. Most of these people are women.

Researchers still do not know just what causes SAD, although there is increasing evidence that it may have something to do with the effect of light on levels of melatonin. Melatonin is a hormone produced by the pea-sized pineal gland in the brain, which is thought to be involved in the way the body regulates its circadian (daily) sleep-wake cycle. This, in turn, may be related to the relatively longer periods of darkness that occur during the fall and winter months. Because periods of darkness stimulate melatonin production, some investigators have theorized that people with SAD may be overproducing melatonin or may simply be hyperresponsive to normal amounts of melatonin produced during the winter months. It is also possible that circadian rhythms in people with SAD are disrupted because they secrete melatonin abnormally late in the day.

Other evidence suggests that decreased levels of neurotransmitters (chemicals that transmit signals between nerve cells) such as serotonin or dopamine may also play a role in triggering SAD. Low levels of serotonin in particular have been associated with carbohydrate cravings in people with SAD, and with sleep disorders and depression in the population at large.

‣ Who is likely to develop SAD?

Approximately 80 percent of people with seasonal affective disorder are women. Why SAD is more prevalent in women remains a mystery, although there is speculation that the disorder may have some connection with female reproductive hormones. At least some of the female prevalence may be due to the fact that women are more likely than men to seek medical attention in the first place, and are thus more likely to be diagnosed as having SAD.

Symptoms of SAD usually begin when a person is in her late teens or early 20s and often—though not always—disappear later in life, particularly after menopause in women. The farther a person lives from the equator, the more likely she is to develop SAD.

‣ What are the symptoms?

Like some other disorders that exclusively or predominantly affect women—such as premenstrual syndrome and postpartum psychiatric disorders—SAD is defined not by specific symptoms but rather by the specific timing of the symptoms. Unlike clinical depression or bipolar affective disorder (manic depression), for example, which can occur at any time of year, SAD affects people on a seasonal basis (although some researchers wonder if SAD may be an atypical form of manic depression without the manic phase). During the rest of the year people with SAD tend to be happy, outgoing, and productive. Because until recently the timing of symptoms was not a standard way of differentiating one disease from another, many people with SAD were misdiagnosed as suffering from other conditions.

Many of the symptoms of SAD are similar to those of depression or hypothyroidism—except that they occur only during the fall and winter. These include fatigue, a tendency to sleep more, irritability, poor concentration, apathy, crying spells, a desire to withdraw from social contacts, and a change in eating habits—in particular, irresistible cravings for carbohydrates. It is typical for people with SAD to gain about 10 pounds every winter and then to lose weight with ease every spring. Other people with SAD suffer from headaches, lethargy, and restless sleep.

▸ How is the condition evaluated?

SAD is essentially a diagnosis of exclusion. This means that it is diagnosed only after a psychiatric evaluation reveals no other obvious psychological, emotional, or social factors that might account for the symptoms. To be diagnosed with SAD a person must have had at least one major depression or a history of at least two consecutive fall-winter depressions.

▸ How is SAD treated?

Recently there has been a great deal of success treating SAD with light therapy (phototherapy). This is based on the theory that light suppresses the secretion of melatonin—and that people with SAD may develop symptoms because of diminished exposure to light. The simplest form of phototherapy is a temporary relocation to the tropics, but of course this is not always practical. Instead, most people undergoing phototherapy bask in the artificial light from one of various devices called light boxes. These boxes, some of which are portable, rest on tables or desks and emit a broad spectrum of fluorescent light that is 5 to 20 times brighter than ordinary indoor lighting and is free of ultraviolet rays. Treatment lasts between 15 and 120 minutes a day, and often can be done at home—although it should be undertaken only by people who are under the care of a qualified clinician.

Another option still under investigation is using full-spectrum light bulbs in household lamps. There is some evidence that phototherapy—or any regular exposure to light—may relieve symptoms in as many as 4 out of 5 people with SAD, often within a few days.

None of the devices currently in use has been formally sanctioned by the federal Food and Drug Administration (FDA), which still labels the treatment as experimental. A light box costs between $300 and $500, an expense not covered by many insurance policies (although patient pressure is changing this in some cases). There may also be side effects, most notably hypomania—a mild increase in excitement—as well as insomnia, irritability, eye strain, and headaches. People whose skin is particularly sensitive to light or who are taking drugs that increase light sensitivity cannot use phototherapy, nor can those who have recently had eye surgery.

Other treatments for SAD—sometimes combined with phototherapy—include antidepressant medications and psychotherapy. Most clinicians encourage people with SAD to make sure that they have a balanced diet and adequate exercise. Generally, the newer antidepressants called selective serotonin reuptake inhibitors (SSRIs—which include Prozac, Zoloft, and Paxil) are preferable to the more traditional tricyclic antidepressants. This is because the tricyclics tend to exacerbate some of the symptoms of SAD, such as increased appetite and sleepiness. The SSRIs have just the opposite effect. Also, investigation is now under way to see if taking a melatonin supplement at a critical time of day may help people with SAD by resetting the body's internal clock.

Manic-Depressive Disorder

Manic-depressive disorder is a form of mood disorder that involves cycles of mania and depression. During the manic episodes the person is euphoric or irritable and as a result may be prone to wild, reckless, or belligerent behavior. During the depressive episodes the same person becomes overwhelmed by feelings of sadness and hopelessness. A person with this disorder (also called manic depression, manic-depressive illness, or bipolar disorder) can swing from mania to depression at long or short intervals or can experience symptoms of both at the same time. Between manic and depressive episodes the same person may function normally, sometimes for months or years.

In recent years a certain cachet has become attached to this illness as people have been made aware that celebrated writers (such as Virginia Woolf, Sylvia Plath, and William Styron), famous movie stars (such as Patty Duke Astin), and brilliant politicians (such as Winston Churchill) suffered from this disease. It has come to be associated with creativity, and some patients with the diagnosis fear the loss of their creative "edge" if they treat the disease. Untreated, however, this devastating disorder, which affects almost 2 million Americans, can lead to divorce, job loss, bankruptcy, alcohol and substance abuse, or even suicide.

Manic depression is a chronic illness that can be controlled only with long-term medication. People who experience one episode almost always have additional ones, and without treatment these usually occur more frequently over time. Symptoms may worsen during and immediately following pregnancy.

▸ Who is likely to develop manic-depressive disorder?

Manic-depressive disorder typically begins in adolescence or early adulthood and continues throughout the rest of the person's life. It occurs in both men and women with about equal frequency.

Although we are only beginning to understand why some people develop this disorder, new imaging technologies have already suggested that it involves alterations in the function of certain parts of the brain. Some studies implicate impaired regulation of neurotransmitters, the chemical messengers that help nerve cells to communicate, while others implicate certain hormones, such as those that regulate the way the body handles stress.

Some of these malfunctions may be shaped by a person's experiences, which can produce actual physical changes in the central nervous system and affect the brain's capacity to regulate moods. There also seems to be a genetic component. Manic-depressive disorder tends to run in families, and there is increasing evidence linking it to a specific inherited genetic defect.

▸ What are the symptoms?

During an episode of mania a person may feel immune to the laws of human biology and society. As a result, she may initiate grandiose projects, abuse drugs (particularly cocaine, alcohol, and sleeping pills), embark on spending sprees, engage in risky sexual encounters, provoke fights with employers, and generally exercise poor judgment. Other symptoms of mania include feelings of euphoria or elation, excessive energy or activity, extreme irritability, distractibility, restlessness, racing thoughts, rapid speech, and a reduced need for sleep. A person having a manic episode may also deny that anything is wrong. Sometimes mania is preceded by a period of hypomania, a mild form of mania characterized by high energy levels, excessive moodiness, and impulsive behavior.

Symptoms of clinical depression (which is more intense and longer-lasting than everyday feelings of sadness) include persistent feelings of numbness, helplessness, hopelessness, worthlessness, sadness, and guilt. People who are clinically depressed often lose interest in previously pleasurable activities, including sex, and may consider life so meaningless that suicide seems the only solution.

Other symptoms of depression include changes in appetite; weight gain or loss; decreased energy; difficulties in thinking, concentrating, remembering, or making decisions; headaches; fatigue; sleep disorders, including insomnia; chronic pain; and somatization disorders (in which a person experiences physical symptoms that do not seem to stem from any physical disease; see Psychosomatic Disorders).

▸ How is the condition evaluated?

People with manic-depressive disorder may suffer needlessly because their illness often goes unrecognized for years or even decades. One reason for this lack of recognition is that periods of mania (or hypomania) may feel good, making it all too easy for the person to deny that anything is wrong. Because many of the symptoms are so broad, too, manic-depressive disorder is readily misinterpreted as some problem other than mental illness, for example, as poor work or school performance or as alcohol or substance abuse.

A person who suspects that she or some family member may have manic-depressive disorder should mention this possibility to a clinician and arrange for an evaluation by a qualified physician, generally a psychiatrist.

▸ How is manic depression treated?

Even the most severe forms of manic-depressive disorder can now be alleviated under the care of a psychiatrist or other experienced physician. Often a person in the throes of mania may need to be committed to a mental hospital for her own protection as well as for treatment. Because manic-depressive disorder is a chronic condition, it requires long-term treatment and supervision even when symptoms seem to be under control.

The most common and generally most effective treatment today is lithium carbonate or lithium citrate (which goes under brand names such as Eskalith and Lithonate). These are salts of the naturally occurring mineral lithium and are administered by mouth in capsule, tablet, or syrup form. Because lithium can take 1 to 3 weeks for full effect, sometimes tranquilizers, such as haloperidol or chlorpromazine, may be given to someone in the midst of a severe manic episode. These tranquilizers are gradually withdrawn as the lithium begins to act.

Lithium can prevent the recurrence of both manic and depressive episodes, as well as control mania once it has begun. It often must be taken indefinitely and is as vital to the continuing health of a person with manic-depressive illness as insulin is to many people with diabetes.

Some people stop taking their lithium when they find it stops the glow they feel during periods of hypomania, or simply when they feel they no longer need it. Like medicine for hypertension, however, lithium must be taken even when there are no symptoms. This does not mean that lithium must, in every case, be taken for a lifetime; but the decision to discontinue it should be made with a clinician, who will closely monitor the patient for any recurrences.

An oddity of lithium is that the levels necessary for effectiveness are close to the levels that are toxic. Toxic levels of lithium in the blood can cause confusion, stupor, vomiting, extreme thirst, severe diarrhea, weight loss, muscle twitching, slurred speech, dizziness, blurred vision, and pulse irregularities. People using lithium therefore need to have the lithium levels in their blood checked regularly. They also need to notify their doctor of any significant changes in weight or diet, since these can modify lithium levels.

There is also evidence that, at least in some women, lithium levels may rise and fall at various times of the menstrual cycle. More studies need to be done, however, before any general conclusions can be drawn. A woman using lithium who notices that her symptoms are worsening at different times of the month should certainly consult her clinician to see if dosages need to be altered, and if she is taking birth control pills she should mention that fact.

Long-term lithium therapy can worsen certain skin conditions, especially acne and psoriasis, and may produce swelling. It may also cause the thyroid gland to enlarge in people who have hypothyroidism. This problem can be overcome by taking supplementary thyroid medications.

Although some studies have shown that taking lithium during the first 3 months of pregnancy can slightly increase the risk of having a baby with malformed heart and blood vessels, more research needs to be done before the effects of lithium in pregnancy are known with certainty. In the meantime, women who become pregnant while taking lithium should carefully discuss with their physician the risks and benefits of continuing the drug.

If lithium is discontinued early in the pregnancy, it will often be restarted during the final weeks of pregnancy to help prevent postpartum depression and mania. Again, a woman using lithium should discuss with her physician the advisability of breastfeeding.

Lithium is excreted by the kidneys and may accumulate to dangerous levels if the kidneys cannot eliminate enough of it. The less sodium (salt) there is in the body, the less lithium is excreted and the more it accumulates. For this reason, people with severely impaired kidney function cannot use lithium. Also, anyone with heart disease, problems with excessive sweating, or a diet that involves significantly altered salt intake needs to have her lithium levels monitored particularly closely.

For all of these people—as well as for the 1 person in 10 with manic-depressive disorder who is not helped at all by lithium—alternative medications are available. Usually these involve an anticonvulsant drug such as carbamazepine (Tegretol) or valproate (Depakote), which was recently approved by the federal Food and Drug Administration for this use. Women who are pregnant or trying to become pregnant should consult their clinician about alternative treatment, as these drugs are not considered safe for use in pregnancy.

Many people with manic-depressive disorder find that psychotherapy helps them to recognize manic or depressive episodes early on, as well as to understand the feelings they have about living with this chronic condition. Others find that they are helped by support groups consisting of people with similar experiences. The National Alliance for the Mentally Ill, the National Depressive and Manic Depressive Association, and the National Mental Health Association all sponsor support groups for people with manic-depressive disorder, as well as support groups for their family and friends.

Anxiety

Anxiety in Women

Anxiety in common parlance is similar to worry. But the kind of anxiety that concerns physicians takes on proportions large enough to interfere with daily activities and is often accompanied by various physical symptoms.

One way to think of anxiety is to regard it as a fight-or-flight response gone awry. In this involuntary response—which developed in animals as a way to prepare themselves for danger—chemicals called catecholamines stimulate the central nervous system and produce increased alertness, quickened heart rate, and tensed muscles. In anxiety the physical and emotional reactions are identical, except that there is often no obvious or true danger—just the response itself.

Psychiatrists recognize several broad categories of anxiety disorders, including anxiety states (generalized anxiety disorder, panic attacks, and panic disorder), phobias, obsessive-compulsive disorder, and posttraumatic stress disorder. Many mental health professionals believe that all anxiety disorders can be traced back to traumatic or stressful experiences earlier in life which have been unconsciously repressed and then reemerge in the form of anxiety. Sometimes an immediate emotional stress—such as a serious illness, a death, or divorce—may precipitate an anxiety disorder. There is also growing evidence that a person's biochemistry and genetic makeup play a role.

Unlike the similar emotion of fear, generalized anxiety disorder often involves free-floating anxiety that does not seem to be tied to any particular situation or object. Often generalized anxiety is punctuated by more acute and short-lived panic attacks, but people with this disorder also have less intense, ongoing symptoms that continue apart from the attacks and are not the direct result of some well-defined irrational fear (phobia).

▸ Who is likely to develop generalized anxiety?

Generalized anxiety affects about twice as many women as men. About a third of all people who have it eventually recover, although men seem to have a somewhat better recovery rate than women.

▸ What are the symptoms?

In addition to feeling worried or nervous out of proportion to any actual danger, people with generalized anxiety often experience a vague sense of dread about the future and seem to be jumpy, irritable, and impatient. They may also suffer from insomnia and depression.

A variety of physical symptoms may occur, including heart palpitations, trembling, shaking, sweating, shortness of breath, "butterflies" in the stomach, "frog" in the throat, goose bumps, flushing, dry mouth, dizziness, and sharp or squeezing pains in the chest. Heartburn, belching, flatulence, and alternating diarrhea and constipation are also common. Chronic tension can lead to aches and pain in the muscles or joints, as well as headaches, particularly in the upper part of the head. Sleep problems may lead to chronic fatigue, which can jeopardize personal relationships and work performance. Substance abuse is another common problem among people with anxiety, probably because drugs may be seen as a source of relief.

▸ How is this condition evaluated?

Generalized anxiety disorder is diagnosed in large part by excluding other psychiatric and medical conditions that involve similar symptoms. Although anxiety itself is a symptom of nearly all psychiatric conditions, including depression and full-blown psychosis (loss of touch with reality), most of these disorders have other identifying features that differentiate them.

More difficult can be differentiating anxiety from somatization disorder, in which *physical* complaints cannot be traced to any specific physical defect (see Psychosomatic Disorders). Besides sharing a number of symptoms—including palpitations, diarrhea, flushing, and sweating—these two disorders overlap in many ways, not the least of which is the fact that anxiety seems to increase a person's sensitivity to bodily sensations and decrease her tolerance for pain.

Anxiety disorders are sometimes confused with physical disorders such as hyperthyroidism. Usually the correct diagnosis can be made after the completion of appropriate physical and laboratory tests and detailed questioning about the patient's history of depression, anxiety, and any current or previous stressors, including physical and sexual abuse.

▸ How is generalized anxiety treated?

Anxiety treated with medications called antianxiety drugs (see below). But because drugs only relieve the symptoms of anxiety without eradicating its underlying cause, they are generally most valuable when used in conjunction with psychotherapy.

The most effective forms of psychotherapy for anxiety seem to combine reassurance and encouragement with behavior modification. Relaxation techniques (including meditation and hypnosis) can teach a person how to gain control over normally involuntary reactions (see Alternative Therapies). Some people are also helped by cognitive psychotherapy, which attempts to elucidate the conflicts underlying anxiety.

Panic Disorder

Panic disorder comprises a constellation of symptoms that begin with panic attacks and eventually develop into phobias.

Panic attacks are brief, unexplained, and unexpected episodes of intense fear accompanied by heart palpitations, shortness of breath, dizziness, and other physical symptoms. These attacks are not just episodes of everyday anxiety or nervousness but overwhelming physiological reactions identical to the fight-or-flight response—the body's way of reacting to a physical threat. In the case of panic attacks, however, the threat exists only in the mind of the individual.

After a person has experienced one of these attacks, she may develop irrational fears—called phobias—about having another attack and will avoid situations or places associated with the initial attack. A woman who panicked while behind the wheel of a car may believe that she will die if she tries driving again; a woman who experienced a panic attack while out shopping may refuse to leave her house alone. The combination of this "fear of fear" and of recurring panic attacks is called panic disorder.

Panic disorder can be so devastating that people with it often truly believe they are going to die, lose their mind, or undergo insufferable embarrassment. The fear can be incapacitating enough to keep a woman from running errands, commuting to work, or maintaining normal relationships. The fear can also foster extreme dependence on family members or close friends. About 1 person in 3 with panic disorder goes on to develop agoraphobia, the fear of public places. People with agoraphobia may be unable to be in a crowd, ride public transportation, visit a shopping mall, or even leave their own home for fear of having a panic attack outside the familiar safety zone.

Panic disorder is often accompanied by other psychological and physical conditions as well. These may include depression, obsessive-compulsive disorder, alcohol abuse, substance abuse, suicidal tendencies, irritable bowel syndrome, and possibly mitral valve prolapse. Sleep disturbances are common, either because the person wakes up in the middle of a terrifying attack or because daytime anxiety makes it difficult to sleep. How these symptoms relate to panic disorder—whether each might be caused by some common underlying disorder, for example, or whether some might themselves cause or be caused by the panic disorder itself—is still not understood.

▸ Who is likely to develop panic disorder?

More than 3 million people in the United States have had a panic attack at some point in their lives. Women are twice as likely as men to have them. Full-blown panic disorder usually develops in young adults, although no one is immune. Often the initial attacks are brought on by some kind of extraordinary external stress, including loss of a job, a death in the family, a serious illness or surgery, a divorce, or childbirth. Panic attacks can also arise from excessive caffeine consumption or from using cocaine or other stimulant drugs or medications.

Women who suffer from panic disorder before or during pregnancy may find that attacks become more frequent or severe after the baby is born. The attacks characteristically worsen within the first 2 or 3 weeks after delivery, often escalating to several panic attacks a day. Postpartum depression may also develop at the same time.

People with panic disorder show evidence of certain biochemical peculiarities that may make them particularly susceptible to panic attacks. Some investigators have associated panic disorder with increased activity of the hippocampus and locus ceruleus, portions of the brain that monitor external and internal stimuli and control the brain's responses to them. There may also be abnormalities in parts of the brain that normally react with anxiety-reducing substances. In people with this disorder the portion of the nervous system that regulates heart rate and body temperature (the adrenergic system) also seems to be overactive. It is not clear whether this overactivity causes the symptoms of panic disorder or is merely another of the symptoms.

There is little doubt that emotions, thoughts, and interpersonal stress (such as marital conflict) play a role in panic disorder. A genetic component may be involved as well, since panic disorder seems to run in families. Several studies are under way to elucidate the importance of each of these factors.

▸ What are the symptoms?

The hallmark symptom of panic disorder is recurrent panic attacks. A panic attack can involve a host of terrifying and distressing symptoms. These include a sense of doom, a sense of unreality, fear of dying or going crazy, fear of humiliation or losing control, racing or pounding heartbeat, chest pains, dizziness, shortness of breath, tingling or numb hands and feet, flushes, tremors, sweating, and chills. These symptoms can last from several seconds to several minutes, although the attack may seem longer to the person experiencing it. Between attacks, a person with panic disorder has a "fear of fear" that is often intense enough to interfere with daily functioning.

▸ How is the condition evaluated?

Often people with panic disorder fear that they have a serious physical disability—that something is wrong with their heart, lungs, nerves, or gastrointestinal system, for example. They may go from doctor to doctor, undergoing many uncomfortable and expensive tests, looking for an acceptable diagnosis. If patients focus on their physical symptoms and deny their feelings of anxiety, their clinicians may fail to recognize panic disorder as such. A person with panic disorder may be diagnosed as suffering from somatization disorder, a psychiatric condition in which physical complaints cannot be traced to any specific physical defect (see Psychosomatic Disorders).

Nevertheless, before panic disorder can be diagnosed, it is important to rule out other possible causes of the symptoms. These can include thyroid disorders, epilepsy, or heart disease.

▸ How is panic disorder treated?

If panic disorder is successfully diagnosed, it can almost always be cured, either with psychotherapy, medications, or a combination of the two. Just which of these should be used depends on the preferences and reactions of the individual patient. There are several studies under way (supported by the National Institute of Mental Health) to determine the most effective therapy. For now a combination of medication and cognitive-behavioral therapy seems to offer many people the best chance of rapid and effective relief with a low rate of relapse.

Cognitive-behavioral psychotherapy is particularly effective in treating panic disorder. The cognitive part of the therapy involves learning to recognize thoughts and emotions that may underlie the panic attacks. This approach assumes that people with panic disorder have distorted thought processes that provoke a vicious cycle of fear. By learning to identify some of the thoughts and emotions that trigger the cycle—such as a fear of having a heart attack—it may be possible to modify and eventually control the responses to them. The behavioral portion of therapy usually involves systematic training in relaxation techniques, including breathing exercises, and in desensitization (repeated exposures to the situation that provokes the panic attacks, but with adequate social support) to help the patient learn to master her body's responses to anxiety. Cognitive-behavioral therapy is often successful after about 8 to 12 weeks.

Some people with panic disorder find it useful to join self-help or support groups composed of other people with the disorder. These groups are also the least expensive form of therapy available. In addition, psychodynamic therapy—which seeks to help the patient uncover early life experiences and deep-seated fears that might be the source of the anxiety—can help relieve some of the stress associated with panic attacks, though this type of therapy usually cannot stop the attacks from occurring.

Certain antidepressants and antianxiety drugs (tranquilizers) can prevent panic attacks or at least reduce their frequency and severity. Tricyclic antidepressants such as imipramine (Tofranil) were the first medications shown to be effective against panic disorder. Today, high-potency benzodiazepines such as clonazepam (Klonopin) and alprazolam (Xanax) are used more frequently. These antianxiety drugs work quickly and have few side effects. People who use benzodiazepines, however, run the risk of developing drug dependency, although clonazepam has a relatively low addictive potential. The risk is highest among people who have already had problems with alcohol or drug dependency. A newer antianxiety drug, buspirone (BuSpar), seems to work well at controlling panic attacks and has fewer side effects in some people than do the benzodiazepines.

As with tricyclic antidepressants, the high-potency benzodiazepines are usually started at low dosages which are gradually raised and then continued for 6 months to a year. After they are stopped, withdrawal symptoms such as weakness and malaise may occur.

Another kind of antidepressant, monoamine oxidase inhibitors (MAOIs), is also sometimes used to treat panic disorder. Because MAOIs can cause a dangerous increase in blood pressure when used with certain foods and drugs, they must be used with particular caution. The most commonly prescribed MAOI for panic disorder is phenelzine (Nardil).

More recently, a class of antidepressants—selective serotonin reuptake inhibitors (SSRIs) such as fluoxetine (Prozac), sertraline (Zoloft), and paroxetine (Paxil)—is being used to treat panic disorder as well. To minimize side effects, all of these antidepressants are started at low dosages and are gradually increased until an effective dose is found; it can take several weeks before there is any noticeable effect. Antidepressant therapy must be continued for 6 months to a year to prevent panic attacks from recurring.

Because panic disorder is a chronic, relapsing illness, panic attacks sometimes recur even after treatment. Skills learned in treating the initial episodes can often make it easier to cope with setbacks. Sometimes people who have recovered from panic disorder continue to have occasional panic attacks for years to come, but these attacks no longer incapacitate them or dominate their lives.

Phobias

A phobia is an irrational, persistent fear and avoidance of an object, an image, or a situation. It is usually considered an anxiety-related disorder and often occurs as part of a panic attack. A phobia differs from free-floating anxiety, however, in that it is focused on a specific object or circumstance such as cats, spiders, crowds, airplane travel, or confinement.

Many of the things feared by people with phobias do have genuinely dangerous aspects, but the odds of being harmed by them are extremely small. People with phobias fear these relatively harmless things to such an extent that they are compelled to avoid them or avoid even thinking about them—even though they are often able to admit that this compulsion is irrational. The need to avoid the object or circumstance of fear is often incapacitating and undermines the person's ability to lead a normal life.

▸ Types of phobias

Phobias are generally divided into three basic types: phobias of situation, simple phobias, and social phobias.

Phobias of situation. These phobias are the most common of the three types. They involve specific circumstances that invoke anxiety. Among the better-known examples are a fear of enclosed spaces (claustrophobia) or a fear of heights (acrophobia). By far the most common phobia—and one that occurs in women 85 percent of the time—is fear of open places (agoraphobia).

Many episodes of agoraphobia begin when a person experiences a panic attack in public and subsequently avoids leaving home in order to prevent this unpleasant event from recurring. People with agoraphobia often spend years unable to venture into grocery stores, public parks, movie theaters, shopping malls, buses and subways, or even long lines. In extreme cases they are afraid to leave the confines of their own home for any reason. Some agoraphobics do have "obligatory companions," however—specific close friends or family members in whose company they are able to travel about in relative comfort.

Simple phobias. This second type of phobia involves fear of a specific object such as an animal or a vehicle of transportation (airplanes, for example). Some psychologists also consider fears of very specific situations such as darkness, enclosed spaces, or heights to be simple phobias rather than phobias of situation.

Simple phobias are not always incapacitating. If the fear is of something rarely encountered (such as snakes), it is possible to go through most of life without having to face the object of one's fear too frequently. Occasionally, however, a simple phobia can be quite disruptive—as in the case of someone with a fear of flying who must take frequent business trips.

Social phobias. The least common type of phobia, social phobias (also called phobias of function), is evoked by the presence of other people. People with social phobias are deeply afraid of embarrassing or humiliating themselves in public and therefore avoid social situations as much as possible. Among the more common social phobias are fear of blushing (erythrophobia), fear of eating in front of other people, fear of using public restrooms, and fear of speaking in public.

▸ What causes phobias?
Psychologists hypothesize that phobias, like other types of anxiety disorders, arise as a sort of defense reaction against certain traumatic or unpleasant experiences in the past. According to one theory, a young person anxious about having forbidden or embarrassing drives may repress memories of these feelings and then unconsciously disconnect or displace them from the original stimulus. Later these feelings are transposed or projected onto some specific external object or mental image which becomes the object of the phobia. Eventually the phobic person learns (or her autonomic nervous system is conditioned to the fact) that avoiding that object or image allows her to escape the unpleasant feelings of anxiety.

In contrast to these phobic responses, anxiety and panic attacks are usually seen as more purely biochemical events that have no particular relation to a past psychological experience. But that is not the whole story since a great deal of overlap exists between phobias, anxiety, and panic attacks. It is clear that more work must be done before the ultimate origins of all of these disorders—as well as the exact relationship between them—is fully understood.

▸ Who is likely to develop a phobia?

Although it is common for children to have transitory phobias (such as fear of the dark or fear of dogs), most long-term phobias begin in early adulthood. Agoraphobia, for example, usually begins between the ages of 18 and 35. In addition, as many as a third of all people with panic disorders eventually develop agoraphobia, and many also develop irrational fears of specific events or situations (such as crossing bridges) that they think may provoke a panic attack. Phobias of all types are more common in women than in men.

▸ What are the symptoms?

Often the only symptom of a phobia is the phobia itself—that is, an intense, persistent, and irrational fear of some specific object or circumstance and a compelling need to avoid it. If forced to confront the frightening object or circumstance, the phobic person may experience classic physical symptoms of an anxiety attack such as trembling, nausea, vomiting, sweating, dizziness, and heart palpitations. Even the very thought of confronting the object of fear can be enough to provoke these symptoms.

Some people with phobias also have feelings of depersonalization, as well as periods of depression. The depression, however, is not considered a symptom of the phobia itself but rather is seen as a secondary reaction to the lowered self-esteem that people with phobias often feel when they are unable to overcome their fears.

Occasionally phobias can be hidden behind "counterphobias," in which a person immerses herself in whatever activity she most fears. Thus, it is not unusual for rock climbers to have a secret fear of heights or for musical soloists to have to battle incapacitating stage fright. When phobias are overcome temporarily, there is often a sense of inner victory, resulting in feelings of mild euphoria and enhanced self-esteem.

Phobias of all sorts usually occur on a fluctuating basis for many years, with periods of remission sometimes interspersed with periods of exacerbation. They rarely go away altogether on their own, especially if symptoms have lasted over a year.

▸ How are these conditions evaluated?

A phobia is usually easily diagnosed from the symptoms by a psychologist or psychiatrist. It is rarely confused with other illnesses. Very infrequently a phobia may be a symptom of a more serious psychiatric disorder such as schizophrenia, in which case it is probably accompanied by other symptoms such as delusions or hallucinations.

▸ How are phobias treated?

Phobias are most successfully treated with a combination of behavior therapy and drug therapy. In the past, the psychotherapy for phobias was premised on the belief that they represented an unconscious defense mechanism against old conflicts. Thus, psychodynamic therapy was often used to help the patient uncover and eventually control the original sources of the anxiety. Research has shown that behavior therapy, which is focused on removing the fears without much concern for their origins, is more effective. In the form of behavior therapy known as systematic desensitization, the phobic person is incrementally exposed to the dreaded stimulus while using various relaxation techniques (such as hypnosis) to combat accompanying anxiety.

Often the success of behavior therapy is enhanced with the use of antianxiety or antidepressant medications. Tranquilizers, for example, can reduce the intensity of the fear, allowing desensitization therapy to be used more effectively.

Obsessive-Compulsive Disorder

Obsessive-compulsive disorder (OCD) is an anxiety disorder characterized by persistent and repetitive thoughts or actions. Although these thoughts (obsessions) and actions (compulsions) appear senseless or destructive—even to the person with OCD—they are extremely difficult to resist. People with this disorder, which is somewhat more prevalent in women than in men, find themselves absorbed by various mental images or rituals—for example, checking again and again to make sure that the iron has been turned off or repeatedly washing hands.

To some extent ritualistic behavior and routine thoughts are a part of every person's life; civilization might not exist—or at least not be very efficient—without them. Many perfectly normal people feel a need to recheck the door lock before retiring each night, while others worry for hours that they may have nicked another car in a parking lot. The diagnosis of OCD is made only if these repetitive thoughts or actions occupy so much time that they interfere with normal functioning or cause significant distress.

Just what causes OCD remains largely a mystery. Some psychiatrists attribute the disorder to early childhood experiences related to issues of control and authority. Others hypothesize that people with OCD may have some genetic predisposition that makes them oversensitive to change.

▸ Who is likely to develop OCD?
Obsessive-compulsive disorder rarely starts in people younger than their late teens or early 20s. It is not uncommon for people with depression or anxiety to have symptoms of OCD as well.

▸ What are the symptoms?
The main symptoms of OCD are recurrent ideas or behaviors that are unwanted and that may appear to be pointless. People with OCD usually have a good sense of reality and readily admit that their obsessions and compulsions are irrational, absurd, or superstitious. They are unable to stop themselves from yielding to these impulses,

41

however, and become so completely absorbed in the obsession or compulsion that they think of nothing else until they have finished. If they are forcibly interrupted from completing their thought or behavior, they usually experience considerable anxiety.

People with OCD tend to be stiff and formal in demeanor, precise and orderly about tasks, and overly concerned about conforming to social norms. They also tend to be intellectual rather than emotional in expression and are notably deferential to others. When they speak, they often qualify potentially assertive statements so as to make them less offensive. At the same time, people with OCD may be prone to lengthy monologues about subjects of interest, and they will continue to discourse even if the listener tries to interrupt or change the subject.

OCD seems to worsen during pregnancy in some women. In others, pregnancy triggers symptoms of OCD that never before existed. After delivery some women seem to develop OCD as a form of postpartum psychiatric disorder (see below). These women often have unwanted and intrusive thoughts of harming their baby. Perhaps as a result of these impulses, women with OCD tend to have trouble bonding with their infants and try to avoid situations, such as bathing the infant, in which they might try to enact their fantasies. Sometimes obsessive-compulsive symptoms accompany other psychiatric changes such as depression which may appear in the weeks or months after the birth of a baby.

▸ How is OCD evaluated?
Clinicians experienced in diagnosing and treating mental disorders can usually identify OCD in a woman showing signs of obsession and compulsion. Certain obsessions, however, are difficult to distinguish from phobias (irrational fears), and in fact there may be a gray area between these two categories of mental illness. In addition, some people with OCD or obsessional characteristics also have other mental or emotional disorders, including depression or, rarely, an early stage of schizophrenia.

▸ How is obsessive-compulsive disorder treated?
Many people with OCD respond well to antidepressants or other drug therapy, often in combination with cognitive or other forms

of behavioral psychotherapy. In women with postpartum OCD or OCD that has been exacerbated by pregnancy, the antidepressants Prozac (fluoxetine), Zoloft (sertraline), or Paxil (paroxetine) seem to be particularly effective, especially if combined with psychotherapy. In women who also have symptoms of depression, tricyclic antidepressants, such as amitriptyline (Elavil) or desipramine (Norpramin) may also help. Since very little is understood about OCD in these women, however, the final word about effective treatment must await results of the various studies currently under way.

Posttraumatic Stress Disorder

Posttraumatic stress disorder is a mental illness that results after a trauma overwhelms normal biological and psychological defense mechanisms. It can develop in those who have experienced military combat, earthquakes, floods, fires, accidents, burns, kidnapping, torture, or concentration camps, and it is characterized by intense and alternating feelings of vulnerability and rage. The most common causes of posttraumatic stress disorder in women are rape, incest, and domestic abuse. All of these traumatic events have the potential to "victimize" a person and produce a sense of helplessness, loss of control, and even the threat of annihilation.

Although psychiatrists and psychologists have been studying the psychological response to trauma for years, interest has waxed and waned depending on the contemporary political climate. In the last two decades of the nineteenth century, Sigmund Freud, Pierre Janet, and Joseph Breuer linked symptoms of hysteria to psychological trauma. Freud's controversial finding that the specific traumatic experience was frequently sexual abuse and incest much earlier in life was dismissed by most of his colleagues, and eventually by Freud himself (since no one could accept that sexual trauma and violence against women were as prevalent as they turned out to be).

After World War I, interest in "traumatic syndrome" was renewed when investigators began to notice that many veterans exhibited hysterical symptoms—such as an inability to talk, see, feel, or move—not caused by any physical injury. During World War II, some psychiatrists devised methods to help minimize this reaction to combat. It was only the efforts of disaffected veterans of the Vietnam war, however, that precipitated systematic, large-scale studies of these symptoms and led to the American Psychiatric Association's recognition of posttraumatic stress disorder as a genuine psychiatric disorder.

Largely owing to members of the women's movement, who for over a decade had been documenting what they called the rape trauma syndrome and the battered woman syndrome, investigators after 1980 began to include in this category the responses to everyday but traumatic acts of violence against women.

Whatever the source of the traumatic stress, victims (or, as some prefer to call them, survivors) with posttraumatic stress disorder have an increased risk of developing major psychological problems such as depression, phobias, chronic pain syndrome, learning disorders, alterations in consciousness, memory changes, impaired concentration, sleep disturbances, and substance abuse. There is some evidence of immunological changes that reduce life expectancy, and people with posttraumatic stress disorder are at increased risk for committing suicide, homicide, child abuse, and incest.

The psychological symptoms of posttraumatic stress disorder, like those of many other mental illnesses, almost certainly have physiological roots (which, in turn, are brought on by environmental or social stresses). A growing body of evidence now suggests that the symptoms of posttraumatic stress disorder may be linked to an overactivity of certain neurotransmitters (substances that serve as messengers between nerve cells).

▸ Who is likely to develop posttraumatic stress disorder?

Although posttraumatic stress disorder can develop in anyone—and may be almost inevitable after certain particularly traumatic experiences—it occurs most frequently in people who are psychologically or physiologically vulnerable, have suffered physical injury (especially to the head) during the trauma, or who lack social support systems. For this reason, children and the elderly are the most frequent victims. Children are particularly vulnerable because neither their physiological nor their psychological functions are fully developed and are therefore more likely to be permanently damaged.

▸ What are the symptoms?

People with posttraumatic stress disorder tend to numb themselves to all thoughts, feelings, or actions that remind them of the traumatic event. Often they show signs of depression, losing interest in the world around them, taking no pleasure from previously enjoyable activities including sexual contact, and estranging or isolating themselves from family and friends. They have an overall sense of hopelessness about the future. Young children may regress from previous achievements such as talking or toilet training.

Part of this numbing reaction is the development of a "learned helplessness," in which the person becomes extremely passive and stops believing that she has any control over her own life. This can result in further social isolation or excessive clinginess to family, mental health professionals, or other caregivers.

It is also common for people with this disorder to deny the trauma or to intellectualize it as something under control. Later they may relive the trauma in the form of hallucinations or flashbacks that can induce the same fear and lack of control as the original event. The survivor may actually believe that she is reexperiencing it.

Punctuating the "background" numbness of a person with this disorder is a state of hyperarousal in which survivors perpetually expect danger. They are frequently irritable, anxious, moody, and agitated and are easily startled by the slightest provocation. They may develop phobias to situations that remind them of the original traumatic event. Vivid nightmares distressing enough to produce insomnia are also common. Many survivors become fixated on the trauma and have intrusive recollections of their experience that disrupt daily functioning. The anniversary of the trauma can be particularly distressing, and survivors who outlived other people who died during the same trauma, or who believe they had to commit a morally unconscionable act to survive, may be haunted by "survivor guilt."

Violent outbursts of temper are common, especially in survivors who have not acknowledged their experience. Some evidence suggests, however, that male and female survivors of child abuse and incest may handle their anger in different ways. Whereas males tend to deal with their anger by becoming physically aggressive or abusive themselves, females tend to direct their anger inward, engaging in self-destructive behaviors. Rather than taking out their anger on other people, women are more likely to become depressed or purposely avoid intimacy with others.

All of these symptoms may appear within days of the traumatic event, or they may take many months to develop. Often mild symptoms or symptoms that appear early may resolve spontaneously within about 6 months as the person integrates the trauma into the totality of her life experiences instead of feeling that it is the sole defining event of her existence. Symptoms that develop more slowly, however, tend to become chronic or recurrent and can be extremely disabling.

Sometimes people with posttraumatic stress disorder may perform acts of self-mutilation or become trauma addicts, since physical stress can trigger the release of the body's built-in painkillers (which temporarily relieve their chronic pain). Many traumatized persons cope with their passivity, hyperarousal, fear, or chronic pain by resorting to chemicals, and often end up dependent on alcohol or other substances of abuse.

▸ How is the condition evaluated?
Posttraumatic stress disorder includes symptoms of other mental illnesses: depression, anxiety, cognitive disorders, and phobias. But if these symptoms are linked to a specific traumatic event and are accompanied by numbing, hyperarousal, nightmares, fixation on the trauma, and violent outbursts of temper, a clinician will most likely diagnose the problem as posttraumatic stress disorder. To rule out a physical cause such as a brain injury, however, the clinician will perform a thorough neurological examination.

▸ How is posttraumatic stress disorder treated?
The most prominent symptoms of posttraumatic stress disorder can be treated with behavioral modification techniques such as relaxation training or progressive desensitization (see Panic Disorder). Stress management techniques are particularly useful in helping people to overcome learned helplessness, social isolation, and depression and to increase their mastery of the environment.

In addition to behavioral techniques, cognitive psychotherapy can help the survivor come to see the trauma as just one part of a multifaceted life story. Once the survivor learns to feel safe, the psychotherapist can help her reconstruct the story of the trauma. This process of remembrance and mourning is based on the belief that symptoms can be alleviated by putting intense feelings and traumatic memories into words. With the support and encouragement of the psychotherapist, the survivor accepts that she has been a victim and acknowledges the effects of the victimization. Slowly, she decides to recover a sense of control over her own life and to restore connections with the rest of the community. By doing so, she eventually recreates the damaged psychological coping mechanisms and returns to ordinary life.

Some therapists recommend that their clients put themselves in positions of controlled risk, such as self-defense classes or wilderness trips. At this point group therapy with other people who have experienced similar trauma—for example, an incest survivors' or rape victims' support group—can be helpful. Some survivors eventually develop a sense of mission in which they want to turn their tragedy into something positive for the rest of the world. They may become active in rape crisis or domestic violence centers, for example, or become involved in some other kind of social action. It is important to remember, however, that survivors never completely transcend the impact of their experience and may find that their symptoms are reawakened during periods of stress, significant life-cycle events, or anniversaries of the trauma.

Antianxiety Drugs

Until the 1950s, anxiety was treated with one of a number of heavy-duty tranquilizers known as barbiturates. Although the dangers of these drugs—particularly sedation, overdose, and addiction—were well recognized, there was little alternative. Then in the mid-1950s the so-called minor tranquilizers such as Valium came on the scene. These were heralded as a safer, more effective way to combat anxiety. The benzodiazepines in particular quickly became among the most widely prescribed drugs in the United States, especially among women. Tranquilizer consumption—virtually nonexistent in 1955—reached 462,000 pounds in 1958 and 1.5 million pounds just one year later. The majority of these were prescribed for housewives—they were "mother's little helpers," as the popular 1960s song by the Rolling Stones called them.

Although benzodiazepines depress the respiratory system and relax the muscles to a lesser extent than barbiturates, they are sedatives with a strong potential for dependence. Consequently, during the decades following the drugs' introduction, addiction and overdose—especially among women—became a major problem. Current thinking about tranquilizers has consequently shifted to the side of caution, but these drugs still have an important role to play in the treatment of anxiety and panic disorders.

Accurate diagnosis and careful prescription are the key to effective treatment, especially in complex cases in which generalized anxiety is accompanied by depression, punctuated by panic attacks, or complicated by obsessive-compulsive disorder. New evidence suggests that some women in these situations respond better to antidepressants than to tranquilizers.

Finally, whatever type of drug is used to treat anxiety, ultimately it can only relieve symptoms. To address the underlying cause of an anxiety disorder, antianxiety drugs are generally most valuable when used in conjunction with psychotherapy.

▸ Benzodiazepines and other minor tranquilizers

Antianxiety medications used today include the benzodiazepines—such as clonazepam (Klonopin), diazepam (Valium), lorazepam (Ati-

van), and alprazolam (Xanax). The benzodiazepines are usually prescribed only in low dosages and for limited periods of time because
of their potential for side effects, including dependence. A newer
antianxiety drug, buspirone (BuSpar), seems to work particularly
well at controlling panic attacks and to have fewer adverse effects
and little addictive potential.

Side effects from benzodiazepines are not common, but poor muscle coordination and control, drowsiness, dizziness, confusion, hallucinations, and decreased sex drive occasionally occur. Alcohol
greatly increases the sedative effect of tranquilizers and should be
avoided by anyone taking them. Nor should any of these drugs be
used by a person operating a motor vehicle or other potentially
dangerous machinery.

Some especially agitated patients and older people may become
extremely nervous or excited when taking benzodiazepines, in
which case the drug must be gradually discontinued. Women who
are pregnant or breastfeeding should generally avoid tranquilizers
as well. Finally, no matter how low the dosage, all antianxiety drugs
should be discontinued gradually to avoid symptoms of withdrawal—such as nervousness, insomnia, nightmares, or seizures.

▸ Antidepressants

In the 1980s, when Prozac (fluoxetine) and related forms of antidepressants made their appearance, they were heralded by the press,
and by some practitioners and patients, as psychiatric cure-alls. The
result was a decline in both the diagnosis of anxiety and the prescription of antianxiety drugs, as depression became a more common diagnosis.

Tricyclic antidepressants (imipramine, desipramine, nortryptiline)
can be helpful for anxiety disorders that are accompanied by panic
attacks. They are also sometimes used when cognitive symptoms of
worry and apprehension are prominent. Antidepressants have little
effect on the muscle tension or sweating, palpitations, and other
symptoms that result from hyperactivity of the autonomic nervous
system. When obsessive-compulsive disorder complicates anxiety,
Prozac (fluoxetine), Zoloft (sertraline), and Paxil (paroxetine) are
effective, although in some patients they produce nervous system
symptoms associated with anxiety.

▸ Beta blockers

Beta blockers are sometimes tried as alternative antianxiety drugs. At this point there is no evidence that they are safer or more effective than benzodiazepines, and they have the added drawback that they can aggravate depression accompanying anxiety.

The one major exception is the particular kind of anxiety attack called stage fright. Beta blockers, if taken about an hour before an anticipated attack, are often effective in preventing the trembling limbs and quavering voice that sometimes afflict performers and public speakers. A woman considering the use of beta blockers for this purpose should try them out at some time prior to the day of the "performance," in case she experiences unwanted side effects. The beta blockers most commonly prescribed to treat anxiety are propranolol (Inderal) and atenolol (Tenormin). Side effects are uncommon, but occasionally beta blockers can cause breathing difficulties in people with asthma, who should use them with caution.

Other Conditions

Anorexia and Bulimia

These two psychiatric conditions involve disturbed eating behavior that may cause irreversible damage to the heart, bones, and teeth and may be life-threatening. Women with both of these conditions are preoccupied with food and body weight, have poor self-esteem and a distorted body image, and often exercise excessively. Many women alternate between anorexia and bulimia throughout the course of their illness. About half of all people with anorexia develop symptoms of bulimia, and about half of all people with bulimia have histories of anorexia or eventually develop symptoms of anorexia.

▸ What is anorexia?

People with anorexia (also called anorexia nervosa) have an intense fear of becoming fat and purposely lose weight to the point of starvation. A distorted body image leads anorectic women to perceive themselves as grossly obese despite protruding ribs, sunken cheeks, and the evidence on the scale. Although women with anorexia weigh 85 percent or less of the amount expected for their weight and stop menstruating because they lack a critical amount of body fat, they vehemently deny that they are underweight. To lose weight, an anorectic woman may severely restrict the amount of food she eats, and she may use self-induced vomiting or laxatives to purge her system of unwanted calories.

Approximately 5 to 10 percent of people with anorexia die as a result of either starvation or suicide. Most of these deaths are sudden and are probably due to cardiac arrhythmias (irregular heartbeats), although some may also be due to coma caused by low blood sugar. Chances of death are highest in anorectic women who lose more than 30 percent of their original weight and in those who rely on purges to enhance their weight loss.

▸ What is bulimia?

Bulimia (also called bulimia nervosa) shares many features with anorexia. In bulimia, however, there is no obvious emaciation to signal an eating disorder to the world. Unlike the anorectic, the woman with bulimia is aware that she has a problem but feels compelled to conceal it. People with this condition repeatedly go on eating binges in which they eat vast quantities of food without being able to stop. A person with true bulimia has an eating binge at least twice weekly for 3 months, and some bulimic women repeat these binges as often as several times a day. This fills the bulimic woman with shame, because in general she fears losing control over her eating behavior.

Thus, once the binge is over, she regains control over her body by ridding her system of the excess calories. Some bulimic women do this by inducing vomiting, either by sticking their fingers down their throat or by taking emetic drugs. Others use laxatives or diuretics. Still other bulimic women may follow a binge with a fast or a period of vigorous exercise. Whatever method is used, the result may be frequent fluctuations in weight but not the kind of severe weight loss seen in anorexia.

The long-term effects of bulimia are less well known than those of anorexia, partly because so many cases of bulimia are successfully hidden. What is known is that the short-term outlook is often fairly good. As many as 7 in 10 patients completing outpatient treatment programs show substantial improvement, although about a quarter relapse within the next 6 months.

▸ Who is likely to develop anorexia or bulimia?

Over 90 percent of people affected by anorexia and bulimia are women, and most of them are white. Anorexia and bulimia are relatively rare problems among African American women.

Approximately 0.5 to 1 percent of women between the ages of 15 and 30 have anorexia, and 1 to 3 percent of adolescent and college-age women have bulimia. In addition to these clinically recognized conditions, there is a virtual epidemic of "subclinical" eating disorders among American women, many of whom do not meet the strict criteria for anorexia or bulimia but who are nonetheless preoccupied with food and weight. Many of these women diet obsessively and use techniques associated with anorexia and bulimia—such as binging, purging, and fasting, or abusing laxatives, diet pills, and diuretics—to keep their weight under control.

That women account for over 90 percent of the cases of eating disorders is hardly surprising. The culture's emphasis on slenderness in women and their consequent obsession with weight are well known. Eating disorders are rare in cultures where food is scarce or leanness in women is not highly valued. Even in the United States there are ethnic differences in body image and desirable weight. African American women do not seem to be as obsessed with thinness as white women are. In a recent survey of teenage girls, 90 percent of white girls said they were dissatisfied with their bodies, and 62 percent had dieted within the past year. Among black teenagers, by contrast, 70 percent said they were satisfied with their bodies, and 64 percent said that it was better to be a little overweight than underweight.

Women have more trouble losing weight than men because they tend to have a higher percentage of body fat to begin with. A healthy woman has as much as 20 to 30 percent body fat, whereas a healthy man has only about 10 to 15 percent. Throughout most of human history this difference gave women a biological advantage during times of famine by allowing them to store the energy needed for pregnancy and breastfeeding. Today, however, it means that men burn calories faster than women and that overweight men tend to lose weight more easily than overweight women. This biological difference accounts in part for women's obsession with diets and weight loss.

There has been a great deal of speculation about just what other factors—besides a cultural emphasis on thinness and the difficulty women have losing pounds—prompt some women to develop eating disorders while other women manage to avoid them. One factor is occupational: eating disorders are common in women whose livelihood depends on thinness or appearance—for example, dancers, models, actresses, gymnasts, figure skaters, long-distance runners, and jockeys. Anorexia and bulimia are also found in young women, many of whom are discovering that their looks are connected with power and capability. Most eating disorders begin in adolescence or young adulthood, with peak incidences occurring between 14 and

18, and a girl's genetic makeup, biology, family background, and psychology, as well as ethnicity, play a role in her vulnerability.

Some researchers have proposed that anorectic girls may lose weight in order to deny their sexuality or to avoid adulthood and independence (that is, by way of a regression to a boyish figure and lack of menstrual periods). Others have observed that many women with eating disorders are overachievers with high expectations for themselves (and high expectations from parents) and that they have a deep-seated need to control all aspects of their lives. Some evidence even suggests that the tendency to become anorectic may be partially inherited or that some neurological or hormonal imbalance may be involved (whether this is the cause or the result of the eating disorder is unclear).

Being obese or even slightly overweight can predispose a woman to developing an eating disorder. In almost all cases, women prone to eating disorders begin with a dissatisfaction about body shape which leads to dieting and then malnutrition. It is not uncommon for a young woman to embark on a diet to lose a few pounds and to find herself several months later hospitalized for serious emaciation. This may be due in part to certain physical and psychological consequences of starvation which perpetuate eating disorders. People who have agreed to be starved experimentally have developed many of the symptoms of an eating disorder—including a preoccupation with food, social withdrawal, loss of sex drive, and depression. Experimentally starved people also often binge temporarily when they are at last offered food.

Finally, people who have been through certain emotional and psychological experiences seem particularly likely to develop eating disorders. For example, the onset of eating disorders often coincides with a stressful event such as leaving home or losing a loved one through illness, death, or divorce. Many women with eating disorders suffer from depression or have family members who suffer from depression, although it is still not clear whether the depression is a result or a cause of the eating disorder. About 10 percent of people with anorexia have obsessive-compulsive disorder, and about half of all people with anorexia and bulimia report having a history of sexual abuse. Anxiety disorders, chemical dependency, and impulsive behaviors such as overspending, shoplifting, sexual promiscuity, substance abuse, and self-mutilation are common in people suffering from bulimia.

▸ What are the symptoms?

Beyond their striking emaciation, many people with anorexia have no obvious symptoms. There are certain attitudes and behaviors that characterize the illness, however. Unlike people who have lost weight or who are starving because of a medical illness, anorectic women are often proud of their weight loss and complain that they need to lose even more weight. Most anorectic women are physically restless, and some exercise to excess to help speed the weight loss. Obsessed with food, an anorectic may delight in cooking high-calorie treats for family members while abstaining from them herself.

As malnutrition progresses, certain physical symptoms begin to appear, including fatigue, difficulty sleeping, and abdominal discomfort and bloating after eating. Skin often becomes dry, pale, or yellowed, and fine downy hair (lanugo) may grow extensively over the face and arms. Anemia and a low level of white blood cells are common, as are increased blood levels of cholesterol and carotene, a building block for vitamin A.

Other changes reflect the body's response to starvation. Fat stores are depleted, and then skeletal and heart muscles begin to waste away. The metabolism of thyroid hormone changes, slowing the body's metabolism in general and generating symptoms suggestive of hypothyroidism, including intolerance to cold, slowed heartbeat, dry skin, and constipation. Blood pressure may fall, urination may be copious, and life-threatening cardiac arrhythmias may develop, sometimes resulting in sudden death.

Women with anorexia stop menstruating, often before much weight has been lost, and this amenorrhea may persist even after weight is regained, resulting in infertility. In girls who have not yet reached puberty, skeletal growth, physical development, and sexual maturation come to a halt. Unlike many other changes of anorexia, which can be reversed once body weight is restored, a young girl whose bone growth has been halted may never reach her previously anticipated height. Women with anorexia lose a significant amount of bone mass, increasing their risk of bone fracture. Even after they regain weight, bone density continues to be reduced. As a result, any woman who has had anorexia is at risk for developing osteoporosis later in life (if she manages to avoid it in her 20s, which many do not).

Anorectic women who purge may develop other symptoms depending on the mode of purging (self-induced vomiting, laxatives, emetics, or diuretics). These symptoms are also characteristic of bulimia, and result primarily from purging and not from binge eating itself. Chronic vomiting, for example, can lead to irritation, bleeding, and sometimes even tears of the stomach and esophagus, as well as heartburn and swelling of the salivary glands. It can also lead to symptoms of dehydration (such as dizziness, faintness, and thirst) and of electrolyte imbalance (such as muscle cramps and weakness, prickling sensations, copious urination, palpitations, and abnormalities in the heart's electrical activity). Repeatedly exposing teeth to stomach acids can decalcify enamel and lead to irreversible dental erosion. Women who induce vomiting with their fingers may develop characteristic teeth marks on the upper surface of their hands. Abusing ipecac to induce vomiting sometimes can lead to muscle damage and potentially fatal heart damage.

Abusing diuretics or laxatives, particularly stimulant laxatives, can also result in fluid depletion, electrolyte imbalances, and associated symptoms. Other common symptoms of laxative abuse are abdominal cramps, watery diarrhea, and rectal bleeding or prolapse (in which the rectal wall bulges into the back of the vagina because of weakened pelvic muscles). Bowel function usually returns to normal once laxative use stops, although in rare cases chronic laxative abuse can result in a "cathartic colon" that cannot produce bowel movements without stimulation.

For reasons not fully understood, many women with bulimia develop menstrual irregularities or amenorrhea even though they are not underweight.

‣ How are anorexia and bulimia evaluated?

Anorexia is much easier to diagnose than bulimia because the evidence for it is much more obvious. Although anorectic women themselves deny they have a problem, it is not unusual for them to be brought in for medical attention by a family member. Also, a clinician will probably suspect an eating disorder in any woman with an unexplained weight loss.

To evaluate the condition, the clinician will question the patient about her attitude toward body shape, weight loss, desired weight, and eating and exercise habits, and will often ask her to record the foods eaten over the past 24 hours. Other questions will concern previous weight loss and diets, menstrual history, symptoms of malnutrition, dehydration, and electrolyte imbalance, as well as use of laxatives, diet pills, vomiting, and emetics. A physical examination and various blood and other laboratory studies will be done to rule out other possible causes of weight loss and to determine the severity of malnutrition and dehydration.

The procedure is similar if a clinician suspects that the problem may be bulimia, although this eating disorder often escapes detection. A clinician may suspect it in a woman who is preoccupied with weight and food or has a history of frequent weight fluctuations. Other hints are the patient's complaints about symptoms that result from dehydration or electrolyte imbalance or certain tell-tale signs such as enlarged salivary glands, erosion of dental enamel, or scars on the top of the hand that has been used to induce vomiting. Some women who would be ashamed to volunteer that they have a problem will reluctantly admit that they need help if asked directly.

▸ How are anorexia and bulimia treated?

Treating eating disorders is often a challenge because so many people with anorexia and bulimia deny that they have a problem—and often behave angrily or manipulatively toward those trying to help them. In addition, a successful treatment program not only has to help the patient regain weight and overcome the consequences of malnutrition but also must help her learn to control her abnormal eating behavior and prevent relapse by addressing underlying psychological and family problems. The best way to accomplish all of these goals is a multidisciplinary treatment approach involving a team of clinicians who together can address the medical, nutritional, and psychological aspects of eating disorders.

When it comes to anorexia, this treatment often must take place in a hospital setting—ideally in a psychiatric unit that specializes in treating eating disorders and can monitor any medical problems that develop in the course of treatment. Usually patients can be induced to gain weight with a normal diet, although sometimes they must first be force-fed through an intravenous line or a nasogastric tube. Patients hospitalized for the treatment of anorexia will also be offered psychotherapy, including family therapy (if relevant) and behavioral therapy to suggest more positive ways to achieve weight goals. Many hospitals offer supervised exercise programs as well. There is still no evidence that drugs—even antidepressants in depressed patients—are dramatically effective in treating anorexia.

Usually patients are hospitalized until they reach a normal weight, although some anorectic women can gain weight on their own if they have close medical supervision. This is particularly true for those who have relatively few symptoms, who are highly motivated to change, and who have a strong support network at home.

Some women may recover after a single episode of anorexia, though more than half of the others repeatedly relapse or remain chronically underweight. Even after recovery many women remain preoccupied with their weight and still have unusual eating patterns and psychosocial problems. As many as 40 percent of anorectic women develop bulimia, and 15 to 25 percent develop chronic anorexia. The more weight a woman has lost, the older she is, and the longer her symptoms have lasted, the less likely she is to recover fully. Women who have coexisting bulimia are also more likely to have persistent problems.

Bulimia is usually treated on an outpatient basis with some form of psychotherapy. Although there is still limited understanding about which type of therapy works best, evidence to date supports the use of cognitive-behavioral therapy. The behavioral component helps patients monitor and change their eating behavior, and the cognitive component helps them change their attitudes toward weight and eating. In some cases bulimia can also be treated with group or family therapy, and many women with bulimia find that support groups (such as Overeaters Anonymous) can be helpful as well. Any substance abuse problem that coexists with the bulimia must be treated at the same time.

These psychological treatments are often supplemented with antidepressant medications, which seem to reduce symptoms of bulimia even in bulimic women who do not have symptoms of depression per se. Among the drugs effective in decreasing the frequency of binge eating and purging are selective serotonin reuptake inhibitors, such as fluoxetine (Prozac), tricyclic agents (imipramine and desipramine), trazodone (Desyrel), and monoamine oxidase inhibitors (phenelzine and isocarboxazid).

Personality Disorders

People who use certain kinds of inappropriate or maladaptive behaviors and thoughts to cope with everyday life stresses are said to suffer from personality disorders. Although such thoughts and behaviors occur occasionally in almost everyone, they become regular patterns in people with personality disorders. They are severe enough to keep the person from working effectively, and yet people with personality disorders often think there is nothing wrong with them. The disorder may not cause dissatisfaction or unhappiness in the person who has the disorder, but it causes problems for the people with whom she lives or works. People with personality disorders are often at risk for other psychiatric disorders as well.

There is a great deal of controversy within the mental health and social science community about whether personality disorders are "illnesses" or just "coping styles." Considerable cultural and historical variation exists in what is defined as a personality disorder; a personality disorder may simply be a behavior that is maladaptive for the current cultural context.

▸ Types of personality disorders

The American Psychiatric Association currently recognizes 11 separate personality disorders. These can be divided into 3 subsets of increasing severity and increasing connection to psychosis (the loss of touch with reality). They are:

- *Trait disorders:* histrionic, avoidant, passive-aggressive, dependent, and obsessive-compulsive
- *Disorders of self:* schizoid, narcissistic, antisocial, and borderline
- *Psychotic character disorders:* paranoid and schizotypal

Some people are diagnosed as having more than one of these disorders at the same time. Despite the name, multiple personality disorder (see below) is not a "personality disorder" as such but a separate category of psychiatric illness in which the person's identity is split between two or more alternating personalities.

Antisocial personality disorder. This disorder is marked by a disregard for the laws of society and for the rights of others. It occurs much more frequently in men than in women and peaks in prevalence between the ages of 24 and 44. It is particularly common in urban areas. Some psychiatrists believe that this disorder may develop in genetically predisposed people who grew up in emotionally deprived or inconsistent homes or whose parents exhibited antisocial behaviors.

People with antisocial personality disorder (popularly known as sociopaths) are typically irresponsible, amoral, and incapable of forming close relationships with others, although they are often outwardly witty and charming. They may violate the law, neglect duties to spouses or children, show financial irresponsibility, commit acts of physical aggression (such as domestic abuse), and act recklessly and impulsively. Typically they have a long history of lying, cheating, truancy, delinquency, vandalism, sexual promiscuity, homelessness, and substance abuse. People with antisocial personality disorder often abuse alcohol or attempt suicide, and they rarely feel guilt or loyalty. To them the world is a cold place to be exploited for personal gain.

Avoidant personality disorder. People with this disorder avoid people or situations that they think may result in failure or rejection. These people actually desire intimacy and success, but they are too preoccupied by worry, shyness, and low self-esteem to dare to attempt them. Some psychiatrists speculate that avoidant personality disorder may be caused by an inability to take criticism, a fear of losing control, or an exaggerated desire for acceptance. Sometimes people who have trouble facing or adapting to new situations eventually go on to develop avoidant personality disorder.

Borderline personality disorder. Three times more common in women than in men, this disorder is characterized by fear of and intolerance for being alone, combined with an extreme wariness of others. The result is often self-destructive behavior—including sexual promiscuity, substance and alcohol abuse, sadomasochistic relationships, and suicide attempts—as well as moodiness and feelings of emptiness and rage. Interpersonal relationships tend to be unstable and fluctuate between clinginess and withdrawal as the terror of being alone alternates with the terror of being dominated by another. People with this disorder often characterize others as either wholly good or wholly evil. They also commonly have coexisting forms of mental illness, including panic disorder, major depression, and somatization disorder (see Psychosomatic Disorders).

Borderline personality disorder is a highly suspect category for many feminist psychiatrists. According to their view, the diagnosis of borderline personality is often little more than a "sophisticated insult." Patients (usually women) who are diagnosed as having this disorder are often dismissed, suspected, or even frankly despised by caregivers. Behaviors that were once lumped together as hysteria are now frequently diagnosed as borderline personality disorder, multiple personality disorder, or somatization disorder, and all of them would be better understood, according to feminist psychiatrists, as variants of posttraumatic stress disorder. Indeed, borderline personality disorder is quite common in people who experienced childhood trauma, including incest and physical abuse. It is also more common in people with a family history of alcoholism. The earlier the onset of abuse and the greater its severity, the greater the chances of a person's developing borderline personality disorder later in life.

Dependent personality disorder. Also more common in women than in men, this disorder is diagnosed in people of normal intelligence who see themselves as helpless and inept, who avoid personal responsibility, and who rely on other people to make major decisions for them. Beset with a sense of their own inadequacy and a need for persistent acceptance, they may fear that expressing any aggressive or assertive impulses will result in unbearable rejection or criticism. Thus, they typically subordinate their own needs to the needs of others, and as a result subtly bind others to them with guilt and indebtedness. Many people with this personality disorder also have problems with substance abuse, depression, and anxiety.

Dependent personality is a controversial disorder in feminist psychology circles because it is a depiction of extreme stereotypical femininity. From this perspective, it simply represents a "pathologizing" of a cultural norm for women.

Histrionic personality disorder. People with histrionic personality disorder use extremely expressive, dramatic, and extroverted behaviors to attract and maintain the attention and appreciation of others. Perhaps because of inner insecurities about their worthiness of being loved or an unwillingness to recognize their own desires, these people are preoccupied with pleasing and attracting others. With their flamboyant or flirtatious clothing, intense or flighty speech, and exuberant mannerisms, they often exude superficiality and insincerity. Relationships with others are emotional but unsatisfying. Many people with histrionic personality disorder routinely attach sexual motivations to other people while denying any in themselves.

People who have relatives with a history of antisocial personality disorder or alcohol problems are particularly likely to develop this disorder. Women are much more likely than men to be diagnosed as having histrionic personality disorder. At least some of the explanation for this may be certain underlying cultural assumptions. Qualities such as "seductive," "emotional," and "charming," for example, are much more readily assigned to women in our society than to men. Some feminist critics have noted, too, that the sex of the clinician can have tremendous influence on these subjective judgments.

Narcissistic personality disorder. People with narcissistic personality disorder are characterized by an inflated sense of their own importance, uniqueness, and achievements. Typically, they are strikingly arrogant, carry a sense of entitlement, and constantly demand attention. Even trivial rejection is difficult for them and often results in either violent rage or deep shame. Regarding dependency as a sign of weakness, they generally have lasting relationships only when the other person is willing to reinforce their sense of superiority.

People with this disorder have trouble seeing others as having both positive and negative qualities. Instead, they tend to rank others hierarchically, idealizing those they regard as superior to themselves and despising those they regard as less worthy. If they think someone else is more talented or powerful, they may become envious enough to resort to ruthless tactics, or else they may find a way to take credit for that person's achievements.

Obsessive-compulsive personality disorder. This disorder is sometimes called compulsive personality disorder, and is not the same thing as obsessive-compulsive anxiety disorder (see above). People given this diagnosis (women somewhat more often than men) are preoccupied with control, rules, and orderliness. Rigid and inflexible, they are obstinate about not bending established patterns and generally fear new or intense situations or feelings (including interpersonal relationships) that may undermine their customary control. While often reliable and dependable, they can also be oddly ineffective—partly because they need to weigh all aspects of a problem before acting and partly because they are so preoccupied by details that they lose sight of larger goals. Also interfering with performance can be a sense of perfectionism, which makes it difficult to complete projects or delegate tasks to others for fear that they will not do a good enough job.

Typically people with this disorder are unjustifiably stingy with time and money, and often are workaholics, valuing productivity or possessions above other people. Finding it difficult to express emotions, they seem cold and detached and can be excessively moralistic and judgmental about other people, for no apparent religious or ethical reasons.

Paranoid personality disorder. People with this disorder, which is more common in men than in women, tend to be suspicious and mistrustful of other people and frequently attribute hostile and malevolent motives to what others regard as neutral, trivial, or even kindly actions. Often this suspiciousness leads them to act aggressively, alienating other people and sometimes turning the suspicion into a self-fulfilling prophecy.

Nonetheless, people with paranoid personality disorder fail to recognize their own role in or responsibility for triggering the hostility of others and often develop a sense of righteous indignation. Apart from having problems with authority or with close interpersonal relationships, however, they are often conscientious and function relatively well. There is some evidence that paranoid personality disorder may be weakly linked genetically to schizophrenia and delusional disorders.

Passive-aggressive personality disorder. These people avoid fulfilling everyday work or social obligations through a technique of passive resistance. While outwardly compliant (if sullen), they subtly undermine a task by complaining, procrastinating, claiming to have forgotten obligations, or obstructing the work of others. Eventually other people become angry or frustrated at their inefficiency—which differs from the inefficiency of obsessive-compulsive personality disorder in that it stems from aggressive inner desires to control or punish other people. People with passive aggressive personalities also have problems with authority figures and may provoke them or blame them for their failures.

Because the behaviors characterizing this disorder appear in only certain situations, some psychiatrists believe that it may eventually lose its status as a full-fledged personality disorder.

Schizoid personality disorder. The schizoid personality disorder, which is diagnosed more often in men than in women, is marked by a lifelong pattern of social isolation. People who are introverted and shy may be predisposed to this disorder, as may people who were ignored or neglected by their parents. Withdrawn, distant, and aloof, these people lack close friendships and generally seem to have little need for others. They often live by themselves and tend to favor solitary activities, especially those with theoretical or nonhuman—scientific, futuristic, or mechanical—subjects. Absorbed by their own daydreams and fantasies, they typically deny physical feelings and avoid close attachments, which they expect will be painful.

Despite the fact that many people with schizophrenia originally had schizoid personality disorder, the vast majority of people with this personality disorder never develop full-blown schizophrenia.

Schizotypal personality disorder. Schizotypal personality disorder—which can sometimes be hard to differentiate from schizoid or paranoid personality disorders—involves oddities of thinking, perception, and communication that suggest schizophrenia but are not severe enough to justify that diagnosis. For example, people with schizotypal personality disorder may have unorganized or superstitious thoughts, speak metaphorically or digressively, or be unjustifiably suspicious of other people. Work-related problems are common, as is social isolation.

There is some evidence that, for both genetic and environmental reasons, schizotypal personality disorder may be more common in people with relatives who are schizophrenic.

▸ What causes personality disorders?

Many psychiatrists believe that personality disorders can be traced to childhood experiences, particularly in people with an inborn vulnerability to them. Many of the personality disorders most common in women in particular have been linked to childhood trauma, including sexual abuse, physical abuse, or both. Nevertheless, it is not uncommon for women to be diagnosed for years as having one or another personality disorder when, in fact, they are actually suffering from posttraumatic stress disorder.

In some susceptible women stressful issues that arise during pregnancy can serve as triggers for personality disorders. These issues include difficulty assuming adult roles, mixed feelings toward the fetus and toward motherhood, the resurgence of unresolved conflicts from childhood (such as differentiating the self from the mother), and changes in body image. Yet pregnancy can sometimes appear to be a solution to unresolved problems and therefore offer a reprieve—though temporary—from preexisting personality disorders.

▸ Who is likely to develop a personality disorder?

It has been estimated that 15 percent of people in the general population have some form of personality disorder, and the rates seem to be higher among people from lower socioeconomic classes. These estimates are questionable, however, since they were based on idiosyncratic or outdated systems of diagnoses. In addition, some social scientists speculate that the rates are higher because people of lower socioeconomic class may be viewed differently by middle-class practitioners than middle or upper class people. Some of this problem will eventually be remedied as psychiatrists increasingly rely on the criteria for the 11 distinct categories as established by the American Psychiatric Association.

▸ How are these conditions evaluated?

Psychiatrists have traditionally been somewhat ambivalent about the personality disorders, partly because so many of them stood on rather shaky scientific ground. Even as better evidence accumulates, the 11 existing categories are by no means fixed in stone. Physicians and scientists as far back as Hippocrates of ancient Greece (who described "the four temperaments") have been trying to categorize human personality types, and today's psychiatrists are quick to admit that the current system is far from perfect. Although the personality disorders can be useful tools in differentiating one problem from another, the specific categories will continue to shift as we learn more about human attitudes and behaviors—and as we recognize some of the cultural biases that underlie our categories.

Masochistic personality disorder is a case in point. The subject of heated debate in the mid-1980s, this disorder was originally formulated to describe the personalities of women who were routinely abused by their partners. It ostensibly included people who kept returning to abusive or exploitative relationships that seemed to be avoidable.

Women's groups and feminist psychotherapists in particular strenuously opposed this category, arguing that it was simply a sophisticated way of blaming the victim. Citing new studies of victimization, they noted that it was the abuse itself that made victims passive, indecisive, cold, and self-loathing, and not some inherent personality flaw. Ultimately, this disorder, renamed self-defeating personality disorder, was relegated to an appendix in the American Psychiatric Association's Diagnostic and Statistical Manual.

▸ How are personality disorders treated?

Patients with personality disorders are notoriously difficult to work with—cantankerous, hostile, or resistant to help. Even more frustrating is the fact that, until recently, most psychiatrists have viewed treatment (which generally involves psychotherapy, sometimes supplemented with drugs) as a time-consuming and often futile undertaking. But, as progress continues in developing better definitions and providing scientific grounding for their validity, psychiatrists are becoming more optimistic about their ability to treat people with these disorders, often with long-term relational psychotherapy.

Psychosomatic Disorders

People with psychosomatic disorders—called somatoform disorders by psychiatrists—show physical symptoms of disorders that cannot be linked to any identifiable disease process or injury. Instead, the symptoms seem to be triggered, amplified, or nurtured by social or psychological crises or stress. This process of developing a physical symptom as an expression of an emotional or mental state is called somatization.

It is easy for most people to accept that physical problems can affect the emotions. No one questions the connection between having incapacitating arthritis and feeling depressed, for example, or the connection between a diagnosis of terminal cancer and feeling afraid. The idea that emotions can affect the body, however, is less acceptable to many people. And yet anyone who has ever had stage fright knows very well the havoc wrought on the body by the mind. Producing tears when we feel sad or turning red when we feel embarrassed are other everyday examples of the mind's control of the body.

Researchers still do not fully understand just how the mind exerts power over the body (or, for that matter, how the body exerts power over the mind). The connection almost certainly has much to do with the many different brain chemicals called neurotransmitters. Emotions may somehow alter the levels of these chemicals and in turn alter the functioning of other parts of the body.

▸ Types of psychosomatic disorders

Among the many forms of psychosomatic disorders are somatization disorder, conversion disorder (formerly called hysteria), hypochondria, and chronic pain syndrome. Some of these disorders have overlapping syndromes and may not be completely distinguishable.

Somatization disorder. People with this disorder have numerous physical complaints, none of which can be traced to any specific physical defect. If there are physical causes, they are insufficient to account for the severity or the duration of the distress. This does not make the symptom or the discomfort any less real, and people with somatization disorder may remain convinced (sometimes correctly) that there is a physical cause underlying their complaints, even if current medical science seems unable to uncover it. People with somatization disorder spend many frustrating years going from doctor to doctor without obtaining a satisfactory diagnosis. As they make the rounds, they are in danger of developing a substance abuse disorder as they are given numerous prescriptions for psychoactive medications.

Somatization disorder begins often in the teen years but rarely after the age of 30. It occurs much more commonly in women than in men, and the risk of developing it is far higher in women who have first-degree relatives with somatization disorder or who have male relatives (either biological or adoptive) with histories of substance abuse or antisocial personality disorders.

Symptoms can involve gastrointestinal complaints, chest pain, headaches, breathing problems, weakness, or urinary problems. Women with somatization disorder sometimes have symptoms of the reproductive system that are unusually frequent or severe. These can include painful menstruation, irregular menstrual periods, excessive menstrual bleeding, and vomiting throughout pregnancy.

As with all psychosomatic disorders, somatization disorder often includes symptoms that indicate depression, including insomnia, poor appetite, and lack of interest in sex. Symptoms of both anxiety disorder and panic disorder are quite common, although they alone do not account for the physical complaints.

Conversion disorder. Previously called hysteria, conversion disorder involves a loss or alteration in some physical function that seems to have a physical origin but that is actually caused by specific psychological factors. It differs from somatization disorder (which sometimes includes symptoms of conversion disorder) because the physical problems are directly linked to some identifiable psychological conflict or need. A woman with violent feelings toward a husband who is cheating on her, for example, might develop amnesia as a way of keeping herself from acting on these feelings. A young girl with an alcoholic mother who neglects or abuses her might develop paralysis in the hand she might otherwise have used to strike back.

People with this disorder are not consciously producing the symptoms. The pain sometimes involves female reproductive organs or sexual dysfunction, but there are other symptoms in nonsexual areas as well. Among the most common symptoms are amnesia, blindness, partial or total paralysis, numbness, seizures, false pregnancy, excessive vomiting during pregnancy, and an inability to talk or swallow. Oddly enough, people with conversion disorder often maintain a striking serenity, termed *la belle indifférence* (the beautiful indifference), despite these dramatic problems.

Although conversion disorder is probably more common in women, it can occur in either sex. Its former name, hysteria, was coined by the ancient Greeks to describe a disease that supposedly resulted from a "wandering womb" (*hysterikos* is the Greek word for "uterus"). For many centuries hysteria was thought of as a physical disease linked to the uterus or, later, the female reproductive organs in general. A woman might go blind, for example, because excessive menstrual bleeding deprived her brain of nourishment. In the eighteenth and nineteenth centuries the nervous system replaced the uterus as the source of the disease, but hysteria was still thought of as a woman's disorder.

Eventually psychiatrists such as Sigmund Freud turned the definition on its head by viewing mental states (usually involving sexuality) as the cause rather than the effect of the physical problems. From this perspective hysterical blindness might result because a woman was repressing a deep-seated conflict: she became blind to avoid having to see something she both desired and feared.

Discarded now by both psychiatrists (because it does not refer to a specific disease) and by feminists (because it connotes misogyny, that is, hatred of women), the term hysteria has been replaced by the term conversion disorder. Today the psychiatric community no longer views the physical symptoms of conversion disorder as real in any objective way. Although a woman with conversion disorder may truly be unable to see, the thinking goes, her "blindness" cannot be accounted for by a recognizable defect in the visual system. The root of the symptoms is not physiological but rather psychosomatic: people with this disorder unintentionally convert psychological or sexual conflicts into physical symptoms.

Conversion disorder most commonly appears in adolescence or early adulthood. People with other psychiatric illnesses—in particular, major depression—or certain personality disorders (such as dependent and histrionic types) are particularly likely to develop it. Some investigators regard conversion disorder as analogous to combat neurosis in men, viewing it as a posttraumatic stress disorder, which in women most commonly occurs as a result of rape, incest, or domestic abuse.

Hypochondria. People with hypochondria are preoccupied with the belief or fear that they have a serious illness despite medical reassurance to the contrary. Like people with other psychosomatic disorders, hypochondriacs have genuine physical complaints—probably triggered or amplified by some kind of emotional stress—for which no underlying physical defect can be found. The distinction is that people with hypochondria involuntarily revolve their lives around these symptoms, which they can describe in excruciating detail. Despite reassurance from health care practitioners, these people remain convinced that they have a serious illness. This conviction is not delusional, however, and people with hypochondria can acknowledge the possibility that their fears or beliefs may be unfounded.

In women, hypochondria tends to develop in midlife, later than the onset of most other psychosomatic disorders. It is particularly common in people with symptoms of an obsessive-compulsive disorder (see above). Sometimes a transient period of hypochondria may also occur as part of an acute grief reaction. Like other psychosomatic disorders, hypochondria often includes symptoms associated with depression, such as insomnia, loss of appetite, and lowered sex drive. Often people with hypochondria also have symptoms of anxiety and substance abuse.

Chronic pain syndrome. Chronic pain can be the result of a number of medical conditions such as back injury or cancer. But people with chronic pain syndrome (also known as somatoform pain disorder and formerly as psychogenic pain disorder) experience pain that is incompatible with their physical abnormalities. In some cases people have an actual injury or disease, or have recently had surgery, but their pain is much more severe or long-lasting than would normally be expected. Others feel relentless pain with no identifiable physical defect at all. Chronic pain syndrome involves pain anywhere in the body which has lasted at least 6 months.

Whatever its source, chronic pain often wreaks havoc with people's lives, leaving them debilitated, jobless, angry, demoralized, alienated from friends and family, and frequently dependent on narcotic painkillers. In at least half the people with this syndrome, the first symptoms develop suddenly following some specific physical trauma. In the next weeks or months the pain becomes more severe. It can be so unrelenting that basic functioning becomes a challenge, and many people stop working, seek disability compensation, and visit doctor after doctor, perhaps undergoing numerous ineffectual surgical operations along the way and taking larger and larger doses of narcotic painkillers for relief. Because these drugs become less effective over time, drug dependency results.

Many people with chronic pain syndrome believe that their pain can be traced to a physical injury or disease still not understood by medical science. In some cases, they may be right, since our understanding of the human body continues to evolve. Still, there is ample evidence that psychological factors often contribute to the pain. This does not mean that the pain is any less real or that the patient is purposely faking it. It does mean, however, that, without the patient's being aware of it, the pain may be a way of coping with some psychological or emotional stress. A woman who feels guilty about putting her mother in a nursing home may develop chest pains after her mother dies of a heart attack, for example.

Chronic pain syndrome can begin at any age but most often starts in the middle years. It occurs about twice as often in women as in men and is extremely common in people who were physically or sexually abused as children. In fact, over half of all patients treated for this syndrome have a history of being abused as children. Often people with chronic pain syndrome also have symptoms of depression such as insomnia, lack of appetite, and loss of interest in sex.

▸ What causes psychosomatic disorders?

Exactly how and why psychosomatic disorders occur has been explained from a variety of viewpoints. In many cases psychosomatic disorders may be symptoms of other psychiatric disorders, including major depression, panic disorder, other anxiety disorders, and personality disorders. In other cases psychosomatic symptoms may be better interpreted as symbolic expressions of some underlying conflict. Some individuals with psychosomatic disorders may simply feel bodily sensations more intensely than others. This extreme perception of pain may be attributable to an underlying abnormality of the central nervous system in the sensory pathways to the brain.

It is also possible to see somatization as an abnormal behavior learned during childhood and reinforced by people and events throughout life. Some women have grown up in families where the only time they received attention or concern was when they were sick. Some model their behavior on that of another family member who used complaints of illness to control others. Through these kinds of situations people learn—usually unconsciously—that to get attention, support, or power, their only option is to be physically ill.

For similar reasons, it is not unusual for any invalid to discover quickly the joys of extra attention and solicitousness, as well as freedom from responsibility, and unconsciously continue illness behavior well beyond the anticipated healing period. Such scenarios are especially common when the direct expression of emotion is discouraged or when having a psychiatric disorder such as depression or anxiety is stigmatized.

▸ Who is likely to develop a psychosomatic disorder?

Somatization is particularly common in women who suffered from sexual abuse during childhood. It is also common in elderly women who emphasize physical rather than emotional symptoms, possibly because our society still stigmatizes mental illness. Sometimes psychosomatic disorders are transient reactions in times of distress. A person who develops a serious or chronic illness, for example, or who is grieving over the loss of a loved one may become temporarily fixated on bodily processes and physical sensations.

Psychiatrists have suggested that people with certain personality disorders may have a "somatasizing personality" that predisposes them to psychosomatic disorders. People with a passive-aggressive personality style may harbor unfocused hostility which produces an illness consistent with their feelings of having been deprived and wronged by the world. People with a dependent personality style may use illness behavior to maneuver themselves into the position of needing and receiving care. Psychosomatic disorders are also common in people with a borderline personality, which is characterized by instability in a number of areas including interpersonal relationships, behavior, mood, and self-image.

▸ How are these conditions evaluated?

A primary care provider may suspect a psychosomatic disorder in a patient who complains about having seen many doctors without being taken seriously or who has a history of many medical tests and procedures for the same complaint. A patient with more than 10 complaints at any given time will also be suspected of having a psychosomatic disorder. Although it is vital to distinguish psychosomatic symptoms from those with a distinct organic basis, often a clinician can do so without subjecting the patient to more poking and probing. This requires listening carefully and taking a thorough history of the symptoms and any interpersonal stresses or other life crises that may underlie them.

At the same time, the clinician will want to make sure that the patient is not consciously creating the symptoms through malingering, factitious illness, or Münchausen syndrome. Malingerers knowingly fake their symptoms for some clear benefit—perhaps to avoid imprisonment or collect disability payments. People with factitious illness—more often women than men—create physical evidence of a symptom, such as a false reading on a thermometer, so that they can take on the sick role. People with Münchausen syndrome, which is quite rare and occurs mainly in men, typically go from hospital to hospital with well-rehearsed and convincing medical histories that serve as tickets to frequent invasive procedures or surgeries. People with Münchausen syndrome and factitious illness often have severe psychiatric problems and should be evaluated by a psychiatrist.

Once a psychosomatic disorder has been diagnosed, the clinician will want to determine if the patient has a history of childhood sexual abuse so that appropriate therapy can be initiated. An evaluation will be done to see if the patient may be simultaneously suffering from any other emotional disorder.

▸ How are psychosomatic disorders treated?
People with psychosomatic disorders are notorious for going from doctor to doctor without finding satisfactory care. This is often distressing not only to the patient but to her doctors as well, who may feel aversion, fear, guilt, inadequacy, and even malice when they realize they are incapable of helping. If the patient also has a personality disorder, these negative reactions may be even stronger. So long as these feelings are guarded against, however, supportive and effective care is possible.

A woman with a psychosomatic disorder should seek a physician who will take her symptoms seriously and work with her as a partner to help relieve—but not necessarily cure—them. While accepting the presence or severity of symptoms, this doctor will also provide reassurance that there does not appear to be any degenerative or life-threatening disease underlying the symptoms.

Psychosomatic disorders are not usually treated with psychotherapeutic drugs unless they are associated with some other clearly defined mental or emotional disorder (such as major depression, generalized anxiety disorder, obsessive-compulsive disorder, or panic disorder) which requires this treatment. If necessary, drugs may help relieve specific physical symptoms. In most cases, however, psychotherapy is the treatment of choice if the patient can accept the association between emotions and physical complaints.

If the disorder developed following a recent psychological crisis, the patient will probably respond well to reassurance and education about how to handle emotional reactions to life stresses. Recovery usually occurs quickly. It is more difficult to treat women who have a lifelong history of somatization; but the value in having an objective, caring person to listen empathetically to problems cannot be overemphasized. Therapists generally strive to help the patient learn to live with the symptoms, improve function at home and at work, and avoid unnecessary surgery as well as dependence on potentially addictive medications (such as narcotics and benzodiazepines) that may be prescribed to treat some of the symptoms of these disorders. In addition, the therapist will help hone coping and socialization skills and provide insight into the connection between emotions and physical symptoms.

Usually hypochondria, like other psychosomatic disorders, is treated with psychotherapy rather than drugs. Perhaps because hypochondria may be a form of obsessive-compulsive disorder, antidepressants such as fluoxetine (Prozac), sertraline (Zoloft), paroxetine (Paxil), or clomipramine (Anafranil) are also sometimes successful in treating it.

Because so many people with chronic pain syndrome have symptoms of depression, they are often treated with antidepressant medications as well. Most physicians do not prescribe narcotic painkillers because their use can lead to dependency, and over time they become ineffective at relieving the pain. Both cognitive and behavioral psychotherapy can sometimes help alter the perception and response to pain.

In recent years numerous pain management centers and clinics have opened throughout the United States which allow people with chronic pain to work with a multidisciplinary team of specialists. In addition to traditional psychotherapy, pain centers offer physical and occupational therapy as well as medical procedures to help control pain. For example, researchers have had some success in reducing chronic pain with electrical stimulation. In this procedure a neurosurgeon inserts an electrode into the part of the brain called the thalamus and moves it around until the patient feels vibration in the painful body part. Then the electrode is implanted in that specific place and attached to a small pulse generator implanted under the collarbone. By waving a magnet past this pulse generator, the patient can initiate a pulse of electricity at any time, apparently providing considerable relief. Alternative techniques to manage stress and control pain, including biofeedback, relaxation therapy, hypnosis, and acupuncture, are often available at pain centers as well.

Multiple Personality Disorder

Multiple personality disorder (MPD) is a psychiatric condition in which the person's identity is split between two or more alternating personalities. Often people with this disorder, which is most frequently diagnosed in women, have problems establishing intimacy with other people and have histories of intense, stormy, unstable relationships. These same difficulties in close relationships also make them particularly vulnerable to victimization by lovers, family, and caregivers. The diagnosis of multiple personality disorder for many people has a pejorative connotation, with malingering or manipulation suspected on the part of the patient.

▸ Who is likely to develop MPD?
Standard textbooks of psychiatry classify multiple personality disorder as a form of conversion disorder—a psychosomatic disorder (see above) which involves a loss or alteration in some physical function that seems to have a physical cause but is actually caused by an identifiable psychological conflict or need. There is accumulating evidence, however, that MPD is more appropriately understood as a variant of posttraumatic stress disorder.

One study, for example, showed that virtually all people with multiple personality disorder had experienced some kind of childhood trauma, including incest or witnessing the violent death of a close friend or relative. A background of childhood trauma also predisposes people to developing borderline personality disorder and severe depression, both of which often occur with multiple personality disorder.

▸ What are the symptoms?
Usually people with multiple personality disorder have a primary personality and at least one secondary personality. Typically the primary personality is conventional, conservative, moralistic, sickly, and "good," while the secondary personality (or one of the secondary personalities) is uninhibited, playful, irresponsible, healthy, and "bad." There may be many other personalities as well, always

including one personality who knows about all of the others. Whereas the primary personality tends not to be aware of the secondary personality, the secondary personality not only knows about the primary but frequently ridicules it or undermines it. On the other hand, the primary personality may hear voices telling it to behave in ways it considers inappropriate.

There are often a variety of other symptoms as well. The primary personality, for example, may have a number of psychosomatic complaints such as headaches, mysterious aches and pains, and gastrointestinal problems. Other symptoms associated with hysteria—such as paralysis that does not seem to be linked to a physical disorder—are also common. These symptoms disappear when the secondary personality takes over.

▸ How is the condition evaluated?
Multiple personality disorder is often extremely difficult to diagnose. This is partly because the symptoms can be so varied and often suggest other mental disorders. It is also because people tend to deny the diagnosis of multiple personality disorder once they receive it. Whatever the explanation, it takes an average of 6 years for a person with this disorder to receive an accurate diagnosis after entering the mental health care system. Frequently women with multiple personality disorder are misdiagnosed as having schizophrenia (see below), conversion disorder, or somatization disorder (see Psychosomatic Disorders).

▸ How is multiple personality disorder treated?
Multiple personality disorder is generally treated with long-term psychotherapy. If the source of the disorder turns out to be an earlier traumatic experience, the psychotherapeutic process should resemble that for treating posttraumatic stress disorder.

Postpartum Psychiatric Disorders

For women with a history of even mild emotional problems, pregnancy and childbirth can result in worsened or new psychiatric disorders, sometimes severe enough to endanger the woman's life or her baby's. The emotional and behavioral problems that arise after childbirth involve several distinct—though possibly overlapping—disorders, ranging from mild to severe.

The most common of these (and not really a disorder at all) is the so-called maternity (or baby) blues, which affects as many as 80 percent of all women soon after delivery. A separate disorder is postpartum nonpsychotic depression (also called postpartum neurotic depression, postnatal depression, or postpartum depression), which affects about 10 percent of women after delivery (there is some debate about prevalence because different researchers use different criteria to define this condition). Postpartum psychosis, a much rarer psychiatric disorder, is an often dangerous illness that carries a risk of infanticide and suicide and requires aggressive treatment within a hospital. Approximately 2 out of 1,000 new mothers (about 3,500 women each year in the United States) develop postpartum psychosis.

Less is known about other psychiatric disorders that may be linked to pregnancy or childbirth. Women who suffered from panic disorder before or during pregnancy may find that their symptoms worsen within the first 2 to 3 weeks after delivery. Similarly, women who were diagnosed as having obsessive-compulsive disorder before pregnancy may get worse both during pregnancy and in the months following delivery. Having a baby seems to induce this disorder in some women who have no previous history of mental illness.

Despite considerable effort, the cause and exact nature of all the postpartum psychiatric disorders remain unclear, although some researchers now suggest that they may have something to do with rapidly changing hormone levels. The lack of knowledge is partly due to a skepticism about the very existence of postpartum mental illness which has pervaded mainstream medicine for much of this century. Even today the official position of the American Psychiatric

Association (APA) is that postpartum psychiatric disorders are not distinct conditions but rather manifestations of standard psychiatric disorders (such as schizophrenia and manic depression) which happen to be brought on by the stresses of pregnancy, delivery, and childcare.

For a decade or more, however, data have been accumulating which buttress what grass-roots support groups maintain—and, indeed, what most doctors have believed since antiquity: that the timing and temporary nature of postpartum psychiatric disorders are not pure coincidence but rather an indication that these conditions require different treatment than textbook cases of mental illness.

▸ Who is likely to develop a postpartum psychiatric disorder?

Generally speaking, women in their childbearing years are particularly prone to depression and anxiety disorders, but just how these changes might be linked to menarche, the menstrual cycle, pregnancy, or menopause is still little understood. Until recently most investigators attributed the behavioral changes to social or psychological factors. Now it appears that these changes may ultimately stem from biochemical factors such as varying levels of hormones. This information has allowed researchers to begin identifying certain subgroups of women who may be more at risk of developing postpartum psychiatric problems than others.

So far it appears that the following factors put women at risk for some of these problems:

- a family history of depression, anxiety disorder, or alcohol abuse
- a personal history of mild depression or anxiety disorder (even if it was never brought to the attention of a health care professional)
- a history of postpartum depression
- a history of severe maternity blues
- a history of moderate to severe premenstrual mood changes

Stressful life situations—such as marital conflict, difficulties at work, concern about pregnancy complications, and physical or behavioral problems of the newborn—can increase the risk for women who, for whatever reason, are genetically or biologically vulnerable to postpartum psychiatric disorders. Another source of stress is a feeling of loss experienced by some new mothers—the loss of the woman's former life, roles, identity, and relationship with her partner. Some investigators think that postpartum depression which begins 4 or more months after delivery may be triggered by these "life event stressors"; depression that sets in earlier is less likely to be a reaction to these factors.

▸ What are the symptoms?

Women with maternity blues have brief and self-limiting episodes of weeping, anxiety, mood changes, loss of appetite, and irritability. The blues begin 2 or 3 days after delivery and disappear within about 2 weeks. Although symptoms may occasionally continue for 4 or 5 weeks, some researchers suspect that women who have these longer-lasting blues may be prone to develop more severe psychiatric disorders in subsequent pregnancies.

Postpartum nonpsychotic depression may involve symptoms similar to maternity blues, but these generally begin at least a week or so after delivery. In fact, new mothers with this disorder may feel relatively well before symptoms begin, and some may not even develop symptoms for 6 to 8 weeks or even longer (there is still no consensus about whether depression that develops months after delivery should still be considered "postpartum"). Symptoms may last for over a year and may recur with subsequent pregnancies. Even though there is usually noticeable improvement from month to month, symptoms frequently flare up just before a menstrual period.

Common symptoms of postpartum depression are sleep disorders, panic attacks, poor concentration, and sometimes hostility or thoughts of suicide. Some new mothers have recurrent guilt feelings and blame themselves for being unhappy with motherhood, for not wanting to be left alone with the baby, for having fears about the baby's safety, for frequently calling the pediatrician, and even for their inability to be reassured. Sometimes there are physical symptoms as well, such as irregular menstrual periods, anemia, weakness, pallor, and gastrointestinal disorders.

Women with postpartum nonpsychotic depression have been known to harm themselves. This is a particular danger because so many people, including health care practitioners, assume that "the maternal instinct" guarantees that all mothers will protect themselves for the sake of the baby. In reality, many new mothers may be driven to desperate behavior because they feel insecure about their maternal abilities, especially if they have unrealistic expectations about what a good mother should be or do. This is particularly true of women from dysfunctional families. They may desperately want everything to be better for their newborn than it was for them but find such fantasies of perfection impossible to fulfill. A depressive disorder only fuels these feelings of failure.

Even more dangerous to both mother and child is postpartum psychosis, in which mothers actually lose touch with reality. This disease is often easily confused with the much milder maternity blues because for the first 48 hours after the baby's birth the only symptoms of psychosis are simple restlessness or insomnia, which hospital personnel and the new mothers themselves often chalk up to the excitement of having a new baby. Today, when the typical hospital stay for noncesarean births is about 2 days or less, this means that the full-blown disease does not develop until after the woman goes home. Here she may still function normally most of the time or feel only slightly depressed; but suddenly she may experience periods of paranoia, confusion, disorientation, incoherence, irrationality, agitation, nightmares, delusions, delirium, hallucinations, or thoughts (and deeds) of harming herself or her infant. Appropriately treated, symptoms often disappear within 2 months, but there is a very high risk that the psychosis will recur after future pregnancies.

New mothers with obsessive-compulsive disorder may dwell obsessively on vivid thoughts of harming their babies—throwing them from a window, drowning them, or suffocating them. It is important to remember that thinking is still very different from doing, and, unlike women with postpartum psychosis, women with obsessive-compulsive disorder do not seem prone to act on their thoughts. Some may neglect their babies, however, perhaps in an attempt to keep from enacting their fantasies.

Women who suffered from panic disorder before pregnancy may

find that their panic attacks increase or worsen after delivery. These attacks involve chest pain or tightness, tremulousness, sweating, palpitations, hyperventilation, tingling in hands and feet, numbness around the mouth, dizziness, feelings of unreality, a sense of being detached, a fear of losing control, or a sense of doom. The attacks generally begin within the first 2 or 3 weeks after delivery, often escalating to several attacks a day. This can lead to anxiety, inability to perform normal functions, and, sometimes, a depressive disorder.

▸ How are these conditions evaluated?

More and more health care practitioners are beginning to look for risk factors as early as the first prenatal visit. Women found to be in a high-risk group may be given the name of a psychiatrist available to provide care after delivery if necessary. This is a lot easier than finding a psychiatrist later, when one is in the throes of a crisis.

As the pregnancy progresses, the health care practitioner may ask about any mood changes or swings, anxiety, irritability, tearfulness, and sleep difficulties. Some of these may be explained by the physical discomforts of pregnancy or frequent midnight trips to the bathroom during the first and third trimesters. If the patient's situation seems to warrant it, the obstetrician or midwife may recommend that the woman see a psychiatrist during the pregnancy, as these changes may be harbingers of a more severe depression or anxiety disorder.

Health care practitioners will also be on the lookout for signs of illness at the 6-week postpartum visit. A woman who has symptoms of these disorders should not let the practitioner focus only on physical recovery, nor should she be embarrassed to tell a doctor that things are "not that great."

Psychiatrists evaluating postpartum psychiatric disorders must first differentiate them from other psychiatric disorders such as manic depression which do not stem from pregnancy. In addition, they will do a test of thyroid function. This is because about 2 to 4 percent of women in the postpartum period develop hypothyroidism, the symptoms of which can resemble those of postpartum nonpsychotic depression. Women with depression will also be evaluated for the severity of symptoms and suicide risk.

▸ How are postpartum psychiatric disorders treated?

Over the years, women with postpartum psychiatric disorders have gone from doctor to doctor looking for someone to give a name to their illness. If symptoms were particularly severe they may have been diagnosed as having a chronic psychiatric condition requiring years of drugs, psychiatric care, and, sometimes, institutionalization. In the past decade or so, however, various support and self-help groups have made it much easier for new mothers to find appropriate care and reassurance. These groups provide "warm lines" through which women can talk to fellow sufferers. They also recommend doctors who recognize that postpartum psychiatric disorders are temporary physiological illnesses related to pregnancy.

Reassurance and support are usually sufficient help for women with maternity blues. Often new mothers need the encouragement of others to give in to what they consider to be "selfish" needs. Many women feel they are "failures" as mothers if they accept help with meals, laundry, or errands, or if they let another family member give the baby a bottle so that they can get some sleep—vital to both mental and physical health. Hard as it is, new mothers must try putting these feelings aside and accept any and all offers of help during the vulnerable week or so after a birth (accepting, for example, that an occasional bottle is not detrimental to the breastfeeding relationship).

The more severe postpartum psychiatric disorders (depression, psychosis, obsessive-compulsive disorder, and panic disorders) are all treated not only with drugs and psychotherapy but also by taking precautions to promote the safety of both the mother and the baby. Depending on the specific symptoms, the psychiatrist may prescribe antidepressant, antianxiety, or antipsychotic medications. These are usually continued for at least a year and then tapered off to avoid relapse.

Selecting just the right drug or combination of drugs involves considering not only the health and safety of the mother but also the health, behavior, and development of the infant. Doses should be kept as low as possible to allow the mother to care for the baby. Nursing mothers should ask the doctor if there are any known ill effects of the drug on the baby. Because many of the drugs used to treat psychiatric disorders are considered unsafe for use during breastfeeding, it may be necessary to switch to bottles. Women taking antidepressants should avoid taking birth control pills, since they can aggravate symptoms of depression. A woman who is being treated for depression and who wants to become pregnant should discuss her medications and plans with her clinician.

Despite frequent publicity and numerous studies, there is still no good evidence that progesterone suppositories have any effect on postpartum mental illness.

If drugs are ineffective in treating either depression or psychosis, electroconvulsive therapy is occasionally needed. Also helpful is psychotherapy for both the woman and her partner. Besides providing support and education, therapy can help open up communication between the couple at a time that is stressful for all parents of infants, even those who are not suffering from psychiatric disorders. Behavioral psychotherapy may be particularly helpful for women with postpartum panic disorders.

Ensuring the safety of mother and child is a vital part of treatment. When a woman with a serious postpartum psychiatric disorder cannot obtain supportive care at home, she may have to be hospitalized. One major drawback to this strategy is that most hospitals will not allow the baby to stay with the mother. This can actually hinder recovery by increasing the woman's guilt feelings and interfering with the mother-child relationship. For years the English (who have also been more ready to recognize postpartum psychiatric disorders as genuine and distinct conditions) have provided mother-baby units so that mothers can be treated without separation from their infants. A few pilot units are now being tried in various locations in the United States but are still not available to most women.

▸ How can postpartum psychiatric disorders be prevented?

Lowering unrealistic expectations about postpartum experience is one way to reduce the risk of postpartum psychiatric disorders, especially the ones that are aggravated by life stresses. This can be done by reading about what to expect physically and psychologically, talking to other new mothers, and participating in childbirth education classes. New mothers should also strive to limit visitors, take frequent naps, and surround themselves with supportive friends and family.

Some researchers have hypothesized that giving estrogen to women just after delivery may stave off attacks of more severe psychiatric disorders, but this theory remains in the experimental stage.

Schizophrenia

The most chronic and disabling of all mental illnesses, schizophrenia is a complex and still poorly understood condition that involves severely disturbed moods, thoughts, and behaviors. It can take a variety of forms, leading many investigators to speculate that the term schizophrenia may encompass several distinct disorders with different causes. In all cases, however, schizophrenia is characterized by psychotic episodes in which a person loses touch with reality or is incapable of distinguishing real from unreal experiences. The National Institute of Mental Health estimates that nearly 3 million Americans will develop schizophrenia during the course of their lives and that about 100,000 schizophrenic patients are in public mental hospitals on any given day.

Some people with schizophrenia have only one psychotic episode, while others have many but lead essentially normal lives in between. Still others with chronic (continuous or recurring) schizophrenia may require long-term treatment and may never be able to function independently. Without treatment, these people can lose the ability to manage basic needs and often end up on the streets or in jail. People with schizophrenia also appear to have a higher rate of suicide than the population at large. Over the past quarter century, however, improved therapies and a better understanding of the biological and psychosocial factors underlying mental illness have allowed increasing numbers of people with schizophrenia to lead independent lives.

▸ Who is likely to develop schizophrenia?
Schizophrenia appears equally often in men and women. Men usually develop the first psychotic symptoms in their teens or early 20s, whereas women are more apt to develop them about a decade later.

There is strong evidence that the potential to develop schizophrenia is inherited, possibly because of a biochemical abnormality (such as an enzyme defect) or a subtle neurological deficit. Studies of identical twins (who have identical genes) separated at birth and raised in different families indicate, however, that some type of environmental factor or factors must also be involved, since in some cases one twin will develop schizophrenia while the other does not.

Whatever the exact relationship between genetics and environment turns out to be, there is no doubt that close relatives of schizophrenic patients have a higher than average chance of developing the disorder. In fact, a child who has a schizophrenic parent has a 1-in-10 chance of becoming schizophrenic, as opposed to the 1-in-100 chance for a child in the general population.

About 1 or 2 out of 1,000 pregnant women develop a schizophrenia-like (schizophreniform) disorder soon after delivery. This form of postpartum psychiatric disorder does not appear to be inherited but does occur more often in women with a history of manic-depressive disorder or who have close relatives with manic depressive disorder. In addition, about 1 in 4 women with a history of schizophrenia will develop postpartum psychosis.

▸ What are the symptoms?

Before developing psychotic symptoms, some people with schizophrenia may become withdrawn or socially isolated, or show marked changes in speech, thinking, or behavior. The psychotic episodes themselves can vary greatly from person to person and can range from mild to severe. Generally, however, these episodes involve distorted perceptions of reality that can lead to feelings of anxiety and confusion. These feelings in turn may lead a person to sit rigidly for hours without moving or speaking. Alternatively, these feelings may lead her to pace the room or rock back and forth.

Hallucinations (particularly hearing voices), bizarre delusions of grandeur or persecution, illogical thinking, or reduction in emotional expressiveness are all common symptoms of schizophrenia, as are displays of emotion inconsistent with words or thoughts—such as laughing while claiming to be besieged by space aliens. Contrary to popular belief, however, schizophrenia does not involve having a split or multiple personality.

Women with schizophreniform disorder following childbirth may have similar symptoms, although these tend to disappear after a couple of months of appropriate treatment. Symptoms are apt to recur after subsequent pregnancies, however.

▸ How is the condition evaluated?

Displaying psychotic symptoms does not necessarily mean that a person has schizophrenia. Usually a clinician will do a physical examination and run various laboratory tests to rule out any medical disorders that may account for the symptoms. Because some people with symptoms of schizophrenia may have episodes of elation or depression, the possibilities of other mental illnesses such as manic-depressive disorder or depression also need to be eliminated. Occasionally a person whose symptoms do not fit into any of these categories will be diagnosed as having a schizoaffective disorder.

▸ How is schizophrenia treated?

Given that schizophrenia may not be a single condition, and that its causes remain unknown, current methods of treatment are based on the ability to reduce symptoms and minimize the chances of relapse. Despite the success of these methods for many people with schizophrenia, far too many others still suffer from frequent recurrences and live with chronic disabilities that interfere with school, work, and interpersonal relationships. Also, because there is still no cure for schizophrenia, even people who find an effective treatment must continue to use it on a long-term or even indefinite basis.

Antipsychotic medications (neuroleptics) such as haloperidol (Haldol), risperidone (Risperdal), and clozapine (Clozaril) are the most commonly used treatments for schizophrenia. They are particularly effective at relieving hallucinations, delusions, and confusion, and allow many people with schizophrenia to function more effectively. They do not help all people, however, and are no guarantee against relapse: about 40 percent of people using antipsychotic medications will have a relapse within 2 years of discharge from the hospital. Even so, this rate compares favorably with an 80 percent chance of relapse in people who do not use the drugs. For this reason, antipsychotic drugs should never be discontinued without the advice and supervision of a clinician.

Occasionally people who use antipsychotic medications for many years develop a condition called tardive dyskinesia. This irreversible neurological condition involves involuntary movements, usually of the mouth, tongue, and lips. The potential for the disabling effects of tardive dyskinesia must be weighed against the disruptive effects of schizophrenic symptoms. During pregnancy and breastfeeding, too, the benefits of controlling the schizophrenia should be taken into account, as well as risks to the fetus or nursing infant.

Lobotomy, a brain operation that was once used to treat people with severe schizophrenia, is now extremely rare. There is no evidence that hemodialysis (a blood-cleansing method used in some kidney disorders) or large doses of vitamins are useful treatments for schizophrenia.

The emotional, interpersonal, and job-related problems that accompany schizophrenia can often be helped with various psychosocial treatments, particularly once the psychotic symptoms are under control. These include vocational counseling, problem solving and money management training, social skills training, individual psychotherapy, family therapy, group therapy, and self-help groups, though not all of these services are available for treating schizophrenia in all regions. More information can be obtained by contacting national mental health associations and advocacy groups. For example, The National Mental Health Consumers' Association, a network of self-help organizations, operates a Self-Help Clearinghouse.

Today most people with schizophrenia can live at home with their families and visit a clinic, occupational therapist, or doctor's office frequently for treatment. Hospitalization is usually necessary during acute or severe episodes, but prolonged hospital stays are becoming less common owing to a trend against institutionalizing the mentally ill. People who cannot live at home are likely to avail themselves of halfway houses or other short-term residential care facilities. These offer a protective atmosphere and close monitoring without completely disrupting a person's contact with family and community.

Alzheimer's Disease

Alzheimer's disease is a progressive, degenerative disease—or, more accurately, group of disorders—that results in impaired memory, thinking, and behavior. It afflicts approximately 4 million Americans and as many as 15 million people worldwide. According to the Office of Research on Women's Health at the National Institutes of Health, Alzheimer's disease is more prevalent among women than among men, and this prevalence increases with age.

Alzheimer's disease is the most common cause of dementia, which is not a disease itself but rather a group of symptoms that involve a loss of intellectual function severe enough to interfere with daily activities. Formerly called senility, dementia was once thought to be a normal and almost inevitable accompaniment of aging. Today many doctors and researchers believe that dementia occurs in the elderly only when they are afflicted with specific diseases or disorders. Some of these disorders—including nutritional deficiencies (such as B_{12} deficiencies), drug reactions, depression, thyroid disorders, and alcoholism—are potentially reversible. The dementia caused by Alzheimer's disease cannot be reversed, however, and ultimately results in a loss of the ability to care for oneself. Other causes of dementia, many of which are reversible, include multiinfarct dementia (caused by vascular disease and multiple strokes), Parkinson's disease, Huntington's disease, Creutzfeldt-Jakob disease, and Pick's disease, as well as infections such as meningitis (inflammation of the membrane surrounding the brain and spinal cord), syphilis, and AIDS.

The average person with Alzheimer's lives about 8 years beyond the time of the initial diagnosis, with some people living 20 years or more. However long the survival time, symptoms continue to worsen over the years, and the patient becomes increasingly susceptible to infections and other illnesses, which are often the direct cause of death.

As public awareness about Alzheimer's increases, so do public fears. Many people who misplace their keys or have trouble remembering the name of an acquaintance fear they may be showing the first signs of dementia. The missing information is usually recovered later, often when there is less pressure to remember it, and memory problems—which are neither progressive nor disabling—can be easily averted by writing reminders or notes to oneself. In most cases these short-term memory lapses are nothing more than what some health care professionals call age-associated memory impairment. Such impairment may simply be a sign that one's mental reflexes are slowing down with age, in much the same way that physical reflexes gradually decline. A number of other health-related problems, including fatigue, grief, depression, stress, vision or hearing loss, excessive alcohol consumption, and overwork, can also impair memory function in people of any age.

About 10 percent of all Americans aged 65 or older do have actual Alzheimer's disease. And often it is as hard—or harder—on family members and other caregivers as it is on the patient. In addition to dealing with the grief of "losing" a loved one who is still alive, there is the guilt of giving what feels like inadequate care and the fear of developing the disease oneself. Many caregivers are saddled with huge financial burdens, too, since the average yearly cost of caring for an Alzheimer's patient at home is $18,000, and can jump to around $45,000 a year if the patient is placed in a nursing home.

And finally, in the course of caring for the Alzheimer's patient, many caregivers neglect their own emotional and physical health. The average age of primary caregivers for people with Alzheimer's in this country is 71, and most of them have at least two chronic health problems of their own.

▸ Who is likely to develop Alzheimer's disease?

The risk of acquiring Alzheimer's disease rises with age, although the disease sometimes occurs in middle age. The youngest documented case of a person with Alzheimer's disease occurred in someone who was 28 years old. The early-onset forms of the disease tend to run in families, whereas cases that develop after age 65 (which constitute the vast majority) seem to occur sporadically. People with the chromosomal disorder that causes Down syndrome almost always develop Alzheimer's disease relatively early. And for reasons still little understood, women under the age of 35 who give birth to a child with Down syndrome (caused by an extra copy of chromosome 21, which is often inherited from the mother) are also at significantly higher risk for developing Alzheimer's eventually themselves.

Although the cause of Alzheimer's disease remains unknown, researchers now believe that some forms of the disease—particularly those that strike people in their 30s and 40s—may be linked to the inheritance of at least 3 specific genes. One of these is on chromosome 21, the same chromosome involved in Down syndrome. There seems to be a genetic predisposition for late-onset forms of Alzheimer's disease as well, although more and more researchers now suspect that, as with heart disease and cancer, most forms of the disease result from the interactions of several influences, both genetic and environmental.

People of all socioeconomic and ethnic groups are susceptible, but people with relatively higher educational levels may be partially protected. A study involving 595 people over the age of 60 found that people with the highest educational levels were least likely to be diagnosed with dementia. The investigators speculated that this may be due to the fact that educated people perform better on tests of intellectual ability and thus are not as easily identified as having Alzheimer's. Alternatively, it may be that higher levels of education somehow increase brain reserves and delay the onset of Alzheimer's symptoms for several years. It is unlikely that higher education in and of itself can prevent someone from getting Alzheimer's disease eventually.

People with Alzheimer's disease have certain physical abnormalities that probably explain their intellectual and behavioral degeneration. In brain tissue examined at autopsy, these changes are seen in fibrous tangles inside nerve cells (neurons) and in clusters of degenerating nerves called neuritic plaques. In living patients there is also a diminished production of certain neurotransmitters, the chemicals that send messages between nerve cells.

▸ What are the symptoms?
Unlike various kinds of normal age-related memory impairment, the symptoms of Alzheimer's disease worsen over the years (see chart). Also, although most people with occasional forgetfulness can compensate by using reminders and notes, the memory loss associated with Alzheimer's soon makes a person unable to manage daily work and social life. Above all, the symptoms of Alzheimer's include more

Normal memory loss or Alzheimer's disease?

Average person	Alzheimer's patient	Older person
Is rarely forgetful	Frequently forgets entire experiences (such as shopping trips or meals)	Sometimes forgets parts of an experience (may remember a shopping trip but doesn't remember stopping for an ice cream cone)
Remembers later	Rarely remembers later	Often remembers later
Is not upset by memory lapses	Admits memory lapses grudgingly, only after repeated denial	Acknowledges memory lapses readily, and may ask for help in remembering forgotten information
Maintains skills such as reading and arithmetic	Loses skills gradually	Skills usually remain intact
Follows spoken or written directions easily	Becomes unable to follow directions	Usually able to follow directions
Can use notes and other devices as reminders	Becomes unable to use reminders	Usually able to use reminders
Can care for self	Becomes unable to care for self	Usually able to care for self

than forgetfulness: problems with reasoning and judgment, as well as mood and behavioral changes, always characterize the illness.

Just how quickly the disease progresses can vary considerably from one person to the next. In the early stages the patient may have trouble finding the right word, take longer to react, experience short-term memory loss, and have difficulties making mathematical calculations. She may or may not be aware that she has a problem handling these and other routine tasks. She may appear self-absorbed and insensitive and have difficulty planning and making decisions. Often there are marked changes in her ability to handle frustration and a general decrease in initiative and drive. Family members may try to cover up these problems by attributing them to stress or overwork or may not recognize that they exist.

As the disease progresses, the person will have increasing difficulties with understanding and self-expression, and will exhibit marked disorientation, behavioral changes, repetitive actions, and impaired judgment. She will often seem lethargic or cold emotionally, having little memory of the recent past and not recognizing familiar people while still retaining a clear memory of distant times. Often she will direct her anger and frustration at family members, who in turn may end up acting out their own feelings on her.

Even at this middle stage of the disease, many family members still deny the diagnosis or refuse help. At this stage, too, it is particularly common for family members to begin to experience feelings of loss, guilt, and fear, and to begin to neglect their own health. It is also typical for them to isolate themselves from friends and family as they devote more time to the Alzheimer's patient, whose behavior may be a source of embarrassment which further reinforces the caregiver's isolation. This isolation often only exacerbates negative feelings and undermines the overall well-being of the caregiver.

In the final stage of the disease, the patient with Alzheimer's requires 24-hour care. She is apathetic, unaware of her state of cleanliness or dress, unable to communicate, and incontinent. She has little memory, either short-term or long-term. Eventually many patients will assume a fetal position and gradually shut down their entire mind and body. It is only at this point that many families, exhausted physically and spiritually from the ordeal, resign themselves to placing the patient in a nursing home and often experience deep feelings of guilt and grief.

▸ How is the condition evaluated?

Currently there is no one diagnostic test available for Alzheimer's disease. Consequently, the disease is diagnosed by excluding other conditions that can cause dementia—some of which may be treatable. To do this, a physician or team of physicians usually conducts a complete physical, psychiatric, and neurologic evaluation. This examination includes a detailed medical history, a review of current medications, a mental status test, neuropsychological testing, blood work, urinalysis, and, in some cases, electroencephalography (EEG), computerized tomography (CT scan), or magnetic resonance imaging (MRI).

Health professionals believe that when this kind of detailed examination is done (which it often is not), about 90 percent of diagnoses of Alzheimer's will be confirmed. At present the only way to confirm the diagnosis is to look for tangles of nerve fibers during an autopsy. There is some new, though preliminary, evidence that a simple eye test may one day provide an accurate means of diagnosing Alzheimer's during the patient's lifetime: some studies suggest that the pupils of people with Alzheimer's are exquisitely sensitive to an atropine solution regularly used to dilate the eyes.

For the time being, however, the diagnosis of Alzheimer's remains an educated guess, which leaves open the possibility that at least some of the people diagnosed with this form of dementia may instead have other, more treatable conditions. In actual practice as many as 25 to 40 percent of all Alzheimer's cases are diagnosed incorrectly. This may help explain why older women—who are especially susceptible to other, reversible causes of dementia such as depression, thyroid disorders, nutritional deficiencies, overmedication, and alcoholism—are diagnosed with Alzheimer's in disproportionate numbers. Therefore, it is important for the clinician to exclude other causes of dementia before giving the diagnosis of Alzheimer's.

▸ How is Alzheimer's disease treated?

Currently there are no treatments available to cure or reverse the dementia associated with Alzheimer's disease. In September 1993 the Food and Drug Administration (FDA) did approve one drug, Cognex (tacrine, or THA), which in some studies temporarily slowed memory impairment in some people with mild to moderate Alzheimer's. Patients or families of patients interested in trying Cognex should discuss its potential risks and benefits with a clinician. They should also bear in mind that, until there is a more definitive way to diagnose Alzheimer's, therapy results will often be incorrect and misleading, since some of the patients studied may not actually have Alzheimer's disease.

In the meantime, some of the symptoms of Alzheimer's— including depression, insomnia, and behavioral disturbances—can often be managed with medications. Eating a balanced diet, getting proper health care, and engaging in regular physical exercise and social activity can make the condition more bearable.

This advice applies to caregivers as well. It is important for family members to take care of their own health, and to spend some time away from the constant responsibilities—sometimes called the "36-hour day"—involved in caring for a person with Alzheimer's. This break can help protect them from depression and other health problems. Many caregivers benefit from joining a support group, often led by a professional counselor, or taking advantage of a local respite service such as adult day care, the Visiting Nurse Association, and home care agencies. Local support groups can be found by calling the Alzheimer's Association, a national voluntary organization which not only supports research into the causes, treatment, and prevention of Alzheimer's but also provides information and assistance to both Alzheimer's patients and their families.

▸ How can Alzheimer's disease be prevented?
Until the cause or causes of Alzheimer's are better understood, there is no way for a person to reduce her individual risk of developing the disease. Family members of an Alzheimer's patient may at least be able to assess their risks of acquiring the disease later in life by seriously considering having the patient's brain autopsied after death. This not only allows the pathologist to confirm the diagnosis of Alzheimer's but also helps determine which specific disease or diseases caused the dementia. Knowing the exact cause can make a difference to family members, since some of the diseases that cause dementia, including Alzheimer's, carry a degree of genetic risk Autopsies are sometimes performed at no charge if the brain is donated for research, but they can cost over $2,000 in other settings. Most of the cost is usually covered by insurance.

Violence and
Mental Health

Domestic Abuse

Over 2 million women in the United States are battered by a family member each year, and over two thirds of all violent attacks against women are committed by someone the victim knows. Women are 10 times more likely than men to be attacked by spouses, ex-spouses, partners, boyfriends, parents, or children. One in 3 women seeking emergency room care has a history of partner violence. One in 4 pregnant women is battered. One in 7 women visiting a doctor's office has a history of domestic abuse. Up to half of all murders in this country occur within the family. Battering is an all-too-frequent occurrence between lesbian partners as well.

Domestic abuse can be psychological or sexual as well as physical. Sexual abuse is any form of forced sex or sexual degradation by a family member. In psychological abuse, a jealous or possessive family member may threaten or intimidate a woman with words alone, forcing her to curtail all other relationships and thus restrict her sources of social support. Demeaning comments or outbursts of temper directed at a woman on a regular basis are a form of psychological abuse. Regardless of which form it takes, all domestic abuse against women (along with rape, incest, and sexual harassment) is an act of violence in which the perpetrator asserts control or power, thereby victimizing a woman and limiting her personal freedom.

There are many reasons why women continue a relationship despite a history of abuse. Women often continue to love and forgive their abusive partner and cling to the frequent apologies and promises to reform. Sometimes the impulse to forgive reflects a woman's low self-esteem or an inability to express anger or aggression. It can also be bolstered by ties to the partner—through children or finances—that cannot easily be severed.

Some women feel that it is their personal duty to help their "sick" partners or that their partners may do physical harm to themselves or others if abandoned. They may feel that if their partner would only overcome a drug or alcohol problem, the abuse would dissipate. Often a woman feels that she cannot leave an abusive relationship because she has no place to go and no way to support herself. She may feel that if she leaves, her partner will find her and kill her and her children.

▸ Who is likely to be a victim of domestic abuse?

Women who were themselves abused as children or witnessed domestic abuse by their parents are much more likely to end up as abused spouses later in life—and to abuse their own children. They are also more likely to be dependent on alcohol or other substances, or to have a relationship with a dependent partner.

Women between the ages of 18 and 24 are at the greatest risk of being abused by a partner, although domestic abuse can occur against women of any age. Commonly the male partner is underemployed or has a job that he feels is beneath his wife's occupational or educational level. Pregnant women are particularly likely to be victims of domestic abuse, and often at this time the violence is directed at the fetus. For example, kicks or blows to the abdominal area or breasts are common, as is rape or increased demand for sexual intercourse. In addition to threatening a woman's health and sometimes even her life, abuse during pregnancy increases the risk of miscarriage and delivering an infant of low birth weight.

▸ What are the symptoms of domestic abuse?

Besides the direct damage inflicted by physical blows, domestic abuse takes a severe toll on a battered woman's health, well-being, and self-esteem. Nearly half of the 206 females seeking help for gastrointestinal complaints in one study had a history of childhood sexual and physical abuse, and about half of them claimed that they were still experiencing some form of abuse. Among these women, the ones with a history of physical abuse were 4 times more likely to have diffuse pelvic pain, backaches, and shortness of breath. In other studies, researchers found that women with a history of abuse had undergone more surgeries during their lifetime than women without that history, and they were more likely to have been hospitalized—not just for trauma resulting from the abuse but also for suicide attempts, gynecological problems, and general observation for undefined disorders.

Women who have been physically or sexually abused have a higher than normal incidence of abdominal pain, irritable bowel syndrome, and functional bowel disease, and are more prone to headaches, insomnia, and fatigue. This does not necessarily mean that the abuse actually leads to the physical symptoms. There is a possibility that women who complain about physical symptoms also tend to speak up more about sexual abuse and violence, as well as a possibility that there is some emotional factor that increases a woman's chances of both developing such symptoms and of entering into an abusive relationship. The precise link between abuse and physical symptoms has not been fully explored.

Studies of the psychological consequences of battering and victimization also remain in their infancy. Still, it is clear that women with a history of domestic abuse have substantially increased rates of psychological illness—particularly depression, eating disorders, alcoholism, and substance abuse. Typically abused women have feelings of despair, helplessness, hopelessness, inadequacy, worthlessness, and fear. They are also more likely than other women to abuse family members physically or verbally or to abuse themselves through self-mutilation, self-starvation, or revictimization (returning to a partner only to experience further abuse).

Over a quarter of women who attempt suicide are victims of domestic violence, and some studies suggest that 40 percent of women in alcohol treatment programs started out as battered women. Abused women often show signs of posttraumatic stress disorder, a mental illness which occurs when severe trauma overwhelms normal psychological and biological coping mechanisms.

Women who have been battered seem to have an increased rate of personality disorders, especially borderline personality disorder and antisocial personality disorder. Victimization is also associated with a high rate of psychosomatic disorders, such as conversion disorder, somatization disorder, and chronic pain syndrome (often involving pelvic pain).

▸ How is the condition evaluated?
One recent study found that only about 1 in 5 doctors detected abuse in battered women, despite the fact that many of these women had visited them multiple times. In some cases these women had seen the doctor 6 or 7 times in one year. The problem is that

domestic abuse can be exceedingly difficult for a clinician to spot. For one thing, battered women are often afraid, unable, or unwilling to acknowledge the source of their injuries—or may even deny them to themselves. Many battered women distrust the medical care system and have difficulty communicating with health care professionals. The abusers themselves may also keep women from seeking medical attention, except perhaps for prenatal care or to have an induced abortion (especially after sexual abuse). Women who see themselves as saviors of their abusers often fear that acknowledging the abuse to a medical professional may result in the abuser's arrest and prosecution (as indeed, in some cases, it may, especially if the victim is a minor).

Clinicians are only now being trained to look for these problems and to take them seriously. If a woman comes into a doctor's office seeking help for a headache or fatigue, for example, it is not always immediately obvious that her real problem is forced intercourse or domestic abuse.

▸ How do victims of domestic abuse get help?

Efforts by the women's movement and the victims of crime movement have helped diminish misperceptions about domestic abuse and made it easier for battered women to get help. There are now shelters and support groups for battered women and their families in many places around the country. These groups can provide information about the legal rights of battered women and can advise them on child custody issues. Advocates from these programs can accompany a woman to court if necessary and help her attain temporary or permanent restraining orders against the abuser. Both state and federal victims of crime programs can help women recover any lost wages or uncovered medical or psychotherapy costs incurred while under care for abuse.

Increasing numbers of physicians are learning that victims of domestic abuse need more than treatment for their physical wounds, and, together with a nurse practitioner and socialworker, can assess a woman's risk of future injury, direct her to appropriate referral centers or a psychotherapist, and help her find a safe and supportive place to stay. They can also help reinforce the idea that the woman is not alone and not to blame and that help is available.

In the past the mental health community held that domestic abuse was a family matter and that family therapy was the only appropriate way to treat it. Now many authorities in this area think that this approach is too idealistic. Today it is generally agreed that if psychotherapy or any other kind of intervention is to be effective, the abuser must first be arrested.

Sexual Harassment

Sexual harassment is any unwanted sexual attention in a situation where there is a difference in power between the harasser and the person being harassed. The term has been a part of the common vocabulary ever since 1991, when the Senate Judiciary Committee reviewed Anita Hill's charges of sexual harassment against Supreme Court nominee Clarence Thomas. Captivated by these hearings, women from many walks of life declared that this problem was ubiquitous in workplaces and schools across America and voiced concern that men "just don't get it"—that is, despite all the outcry, men simply do not understand why sexual harassment is so troubling to women.

One of the reasons why many people may have trouble "getting it" is that it is not always obvious just which behaviors constitute sexual harassment. Virtually everyone would agree that there has been sexual harassment when a women's refusal to grant sexual favors to her boss results in her being barred from job advancement, demoted, or fired. Equally clear is the case of a college student who must sleep with a professor to obtain a recommendation for graduate school, or the office worker who must listen to obscene propositions on a regular basis from a co-worker. But most women—and most courts of law—consider less egregious actions to constitute sexual harassment as well. A woman who works in a small factory whose walls are covered with nude pin-ups, the secretary who must endure endless pinches and pats from her boss, and the student who has to listen to off-color jokes in an auto mechanics class—all of these women are being sexually harassed as well.

Just why some of these behaviors constitute sexual harassment seems to baffle many men—and some women. The reason why unwanted sexual attention is so troubling to women has to do with a power differential, perceived or real, between men and women in our culture. A woman who is sexually harassed often feels she has no option but to endure the mistreatment because she might lose her job, flunk a course, or anger the harasser to the point of physical harm. This power differential means that sexual harassment can occur even when a woman is not in an officially subordinate position. For example, in one oft-cited case, a female surgeon and tenured professor at Stanford University Medical School ended up resigning her position after receiving clandestine caresses and being called "Honey" by her colleagues for many years. Similarly, many a waitress has to put up with the leers and lewd remarks of her customers day after day, and these women are being harassed as well—even though the customers are not her employers in any formal sense. Whether a woman is harassed by a boss, a co-worker, or a client, any sexual attention that makes the work environment hostile or pressured is clearly sexual harassment.

Because many men consider sexual advances and remarks flattering, however, or belong to a generation or an ethnic tradition in which such behaviors are accepted, they fail to understand why many women find them degrading or even frightening. Differing perspectives about what constitutes sexual harassment can lead even the best-intentioned people to feel that they are walking on eggshells as they try to determine an appropriate way to entertain clients, travel with colleagues of the other sex, or express gratitude to their subordinates. As women continue to join men in the workplace—working, traveling, and socializing with male colleagues—the old rules about acceptable behavior between the sexes become increasingly outmoded and subject to a great deal of misinterpretation. Lesbian and minority women may be at particular risk for sexual harassment because they are stigmatized groups who are often in a position of lesser status and power than heterosexual and white women.

▸ What are the physical and emotional symptoms?
Sexual harassment not only makes women feel afraid and powerless but also creates emotional stress. This can manifest itself as anxiety, anger, fear, and helplessness, as well as in frequent headaches or problems with drug or alcohol abuse. A few women develop symptoms reminiscent of the posttraumatic stress disorder (see entry) sometimes experienced by victims of rape or domestic abuse. Some women miss days of work because of these symptoms or find that their job performance suffers along with their motivation and their confidence in their abilities.

A now-classic random survey of government employees conducted by the U.S. Merit Systems Protection Board in 1981 found that 42 percent of over 10,000 women responding said that they had been sexually harassed on the job. This study estimated that sexual harassment had resulted in significant amounts of job turnover, absenteeism, and a cost to taxpayers of $189 million in health benefits over a two-year period.

▸ How can a woman protect herself against sexual harassment?

Regulatory protections. A set of guidelines issued in 1980 by the Equal Employment Opportunity Commission (EEOC), the federal agency that handles cases of sexual harassment, defined sexual harassment as "unwelcome sexual advances, requests for sexual favors, and other verbal or physical conduct of a sexual nature" when employment decisions hinge on submission to or rejection of this conduct, or when this conduct substantially interferes with a person's work performance or creates an "intimidating, hostile, or offensive working environment." Six years later the U.S. Supreme Court ruled that sexual harassment in the workplace was illegal because it violated the antidiscrimination laws under Title VII of the 1964 Civil Rights Act.

Charges of sexual harassment in the workplace can be filed with the Federal Equal Employment Opportunity Commission or with a state's Human Rights Commission. In a school or university setting, sexual harassment is defined as a form of sexual discrimination under Title IX of the Education Amendment of 1972.

Whether or not a woman wants to press charges, her first step in handling sexual harassment should ideally be to let the harasser know in no uncertain terms that his or her behavior is unacceptable. This is not always possible, of course. Some women sense that if they confront the harasser directly, the repercussions will far outweigh any possible benefits. Other women have difficulty with direct confrontation, and may find themselves smiling and apologizing even as they chastise. This kind of behavior is easily misinterpreted and does not hold up very well in court.

If filing a lawsuit is a possibility, it is best to document all incidents and confrontations in as much detail as possible, and to save copies of any written correspondence either to or from the harasser. Repeated harassment should be reported to a supervisor or personnel officer (if possible), and information should be obtained about the company's sexual harassment policy (if one exists). Since the Supreme Court's 1986 decision, many companies have found it in their own best interest to institute such policies, since they are liable for sexual harassment that occurs in the workplace and may have to pay the damages, attorney's fees, and even lost wages of any employees who are sexually harassed. The EEOC also encourages employers to raise the subject of sexual harassment actively, issue statements or handbooks to increase employees' awareness, develop appropriate sanctions against it, and educate employees about their rights under Title VII. Sometimes companies that do not have a sexual harassment policy can be induced to institute one on these grounds.

Nonlegal recourse. For all the talk about sexual harassment and recent legal protections, very few women actually press charges and follow through. The reasons are similar to the reasons why many women do not prosecute the perpetrators of rape or domestic abuse. Some women are held back by concern for the harasser: as troubled as they are, they cannot justify embarrassing the harasser or "ruining" his life by prosecuting him publicly. Other women hesitate to file charges because they are afraid of emotional, occupational, or even physical consequences. In addition, many women know that victims of sexual harassment end up cross-examined by a defense attorney as if they themselves were on trial: their behavior in the workplace, their social life, and their style of dress are often held up for scrutiny, as if they had somehow brought the harassment on themselves.

There are a number of jobs in which pressing charges is not really practical. Not all women have the means or opportunity to fight their way through all the red tape involved in alienating an employer, hiring a lawyer, and going to court. It is also harder to press charges when the harassment comes from customers—patrons at a restaurant, clients at a travel or real estate agency—rather than employers.

There are some private steps that can be taken by any woman who is being harassed in the workplace. One is to remember that, whatever others may say, women do not bring sexual harassment on themselves; they are not to blame for being victims. It can also be helpful to talk to other women in the same environment, who often will have experienced a similar problem. At the very least this can result in a support network; at best it may generate some form of collective action against the offender. Sometimes, however, co-workers isolate themselves from a woman who claims to have been sexually harassed, to protect either their jobs or their own sense of security. In such cases it may be better to turn to a women's advocacy organization or local rape crisis center for support and guidance.

Rape

Rape can involve any sexual assault—including but not limited to sexual intercourse—achieved with physical force or the threat of physical force. Motivated by the desire to dominate or humiliate, rape is an act of violence rather than an act of sexuality.

Rape is more likely to be committed by someone the victim knows than by a stranger—thus the terms date rape, acquaintance rape, and marital rape. Rape by a known person is also more likely to result in physical injury. Most rapes are planned in advance, and over half occur in the victim's own home.

In the past two decades or so, the number of reported rapes has been increasing faster than any other crime of violence. This is partly because women are more willing to report rapes, now that some of the stigma associated with rape has been lifted, largely owing to the efforts of the women's movement and the victims of crime movement. But since the mid-1970s an explosion of research on sexual assault has confirmed the pervasiveness of rape and incest against women and children in the United States.

Formerly it was common to assume that women provoked rape or even that they enjoyed it. Law enforcement officials, academic investigators, and health professionals typically minimized the trauma that the victim experienced or blamed her for the assault. Although this kind of thinking is by no means extinct, grass-roots support services (such as local rape crisis centers), rape reform legislation, and even financial compensation for victims is now available in many parts of this country.

▸ Who is likely to be raped?

Anyone (including babies, males, and the elderly) can be a victim of rape, but being female, young, married or formerly married, and living in a city all increase the chances of being raped. Somewhere between 6 and 25 percent of women in this country have been victims of a completed rape, and up to 50 percent of women have been threatened with rape at least once in their lives. Marital rape has been reported to occur in 3 to 14 percent of marriages.

High as these numbers are, they undoubtedly underestimate the extent of the problem, given the reluctance of many women to report rape, especially marital rape. It is generally believed that only about 1 rape in 10 committed by a stranger is reported, and the percentage is even lower when the victim knows the rapist.

Women hesitate to report rape, or actually decide not to report rape, for a number of reasons. They may not wish to turn in an acquaintance or spouse because they do not want to see that person prosecuted and jailed. Other women are reluctant to report rape because they feel ashamed, embarrassed, or polluted, and prefer to withdraw rather than face what they fear will be (and often is) public humiliation and exposure. Even with increasing public support for victims and widening discussion of rape, until recently it was common for defense attorneys to impugn a rape victim's character and personal life. Some women—even if they have been victimized—may feel that their personal life is not the business of the state.

Despite many improvements in training people in police departments and hospital emergency rooms to respond sensitively, the treatment a rape victim gets still varies according to her race, sexual orientation, degree of affluence, marital status, and relationship to the rapist. Only half of all alleged rapists are ever arrested. Of these arrests, only 3 in 5 result in prosecution, and only half of the cases that are prosecuted are strong enough to be brought to trial. In the end, less than 1 in 6 of the cases that do eventually go to trial results in conviction. Knowing that prosecuting a rape often means being interrogated by hostile defense attorneys and accused of seduction in a court of law and that few rape trials end in conviction discourages many women from reporting this crime in the first place.

▸ What are the physical and psychological effects of rape?

Because a rape generally involves force, it frequently results in physical injuries. These usually involve the violated area (genital tract, mouth, or anus), as well as cuts and bruises on other parts of the body. Nausea and abdominal pain are common.

Women who have experienced rape and other forms of sexual assault are at future risk for chronic pelvic pain, abdominal pain, irritable bowel syndrome, and sexual dysfunction. Memories of the assault combined with actual physical injury can result in a variety of gynecological complaints. In addition, women who have been raped face the risk of contracting a sexually transmitted disease, including HIV. Women in their reproductive years may be at risk for pregnancy.

Almost all women who have been raped experience some degree of emotional or psychological disturbance, even if at first they numb themselves to the trauma, deny their feelings, and try to go on with life as if nothing had happened. At some point most women experience anger, fear, insecurity, depression, insomnia, nightmares, aversion to sexual contact, and feelings of violation and loss of control. These can last for months or even years after the rape. An event that reminds the woman of the rape or makes her feel that she has no control over her life can trigger these feelings even after she thinks she has recovered.

Many women feel that they were somehow responsible for the rape—that they should not have flirted with the man in a bar, or that they should have made sure the bedroom windows were locked, or that they should have avoided being alone in the house with the perpetrator, or that they should not have walked down a deserted street after dark. As a result, they may feel guilty and worthless.

It is common for rape victims to develop posttraumatic stress disorder, which results when the mind and body are overwhelmed by a traumatic experience. Sexual assault has also been associated with other psychiatric conditions, including major depression, obsessive-compulsive disorder, and alcohol or substance abuse.

Frequently problems develop with marital or other sexual partners. Men from certain backgrounds may reject a raped woman as "fallen" or "polluted," while other men, though sympathetic, may involuntarily respond with rage or anger directed at the victim, when in fact the woman needs love and support. Other partners may feel helpless and prefer to ignore the trauma by continuing as usual once the obvious physical problems have been resolved, oblivious to the woman's need to talk through her feelings.

▸ What should a woman do after a rape?

The first step to take after a rape is to seek medical attention for any physical injuries that may have been sustained. This can usually be done in a hospital emergency room. Besides evaluating the woman's physical health, the examiner will try to collect physical evidence of the rape in case the woman later decides to prosecute. For this reason—and because of the risk of acquiring a sexually transmitted disease or becoming pregnant—it is important even for women who feel they are fine physically to have a thorough medical examination.

It is best to see a doctor trained in examining rape victims and familiar with the local laws regarding the collection of physical evidence. Evidence of the rape will be more convincing if it is obtained as soon as possible after the rape. Evidence of sperm, for example, can disappear after only about 8 hours. Hard as it may be for the woman, it is important, too, to be examined before taking a shower, bathing, or douching, since these activities can wash away evidence that may turn out to be crucial in obtaining a conviction.

Besides evaluating and treating injuries and recording them in detail, the examiner will look for physical evidence such as blood or hair from the rapist on the woman's body or clothing. The woman's clothing may be kept as evidence, so if possible she should take an extra change of clothes with her to the emergency room or doctor's office. If the rape was vaginal, the examiner will do a pelvic examination and a Pap test to look for any evidence of sperm cells. These can also be used to determine the rapist's blood type. The cervix and vaginal walls will be examined for the presence of sperm or acid phosphatase, a substance produced by the prostate gland and ejaculated in the seminal fluid. If the rape was anal or oral, specimens will also be taken from the rectum or mouth.

▸ How is a rape victim treated?

Although some tests will be done for sexually transmitted diseases at the time of the initial examination, not all of these diseases can be diagnosed after initial exposure. For this reason, some of the tests will need to be repeated later. For example, a woman must wait at least 2 weeks for another gonorrhea test, 3 months for syphilis, and 6 months for HIV. In the meantime, the doctor may prescribe antibiotics to be taken as a preventive measure.

If the woman is in her reproductive years, not using birth control pills or some other form of contraceptive, and near midcycle, the chance of a pregnancy is considerable. For that reason, she should consider taking a morning-after pill. This medication, taken orally or by injection within 72 hours of unprotected intercourse, usually consists of a high dose of estrogen such as is found in some birth control pills.

In the emergency room of some larger hospitals, there may be a social worker trained to support women who have been raped. If the hospital does not provide such services, women should consider contacting a local rape crisis center either before or after the medical examination. Often these centers, which in many places are open 24 hours a day, can be contacted by the hospital if the woman has not already called. Available across the United States, rape crisis centers can send someone to act as the woman's advocate—that is, a person who will provide support and assistance—at the hospital and the police station. They can also provide counseling on getting medical care, as well as instruction on how to report a rape to the police and how to handle the legal process if the woman decides to press charges. Later, advocates may accompany the woman to the lawyer's office and courthouse as well, working at all times to ensure that she is treated respectfully. Similar information may also be available from programs for victims of domestic abuse, women's self-help clinics, or the district attorney's office, as well as through attorneys specializing in family law or personal injury.

An advocate from a rape crisis center can help the rape victim find psychological counseling should she need it. This is often available through victims of rape groups sponsored by the center itself, other community organizations, or hospital psychiatric departments. If necessary, the advocate can also help the woman find a professional psychotherapist experienced in working with rape victims. Teenage and younger victims of rape are especially likely to require this additional counseling.

Whether or not a woman eventually decides to press charges, she should carefully consider reporting the rape to the police as soon as her medical needs have been met. At the police station she will be asked to describe in detail what happened and to describe and identify the attacker as specifically as possible so that he can be arrested.

Prompt reporting will greatly improve the woman's case should she decide to press charges.

For those women who may not be willing to have an acquaintance or partner arrested, or who for whatever reason do not wish to make the rape a matter of public record, many states now allow women to report a rape anonymously. This allows police to keep records of the crime and provide support for the victim but still gives her time to decide if she wants to identify herself and the rapist and press charges against him. More specific information on local provisions can be obtained through a local rape crisis center.

▸ How can rape be prevented?

The notion of preventing rape is specious in the sense that it implies that rape can be avoided and that victims are somehow to blame if it is not. Because the majority of rapes are committed in the home by someone the victim knows, many of the safety measures routinely suggested are of little value. Still, the realities of modern life demand that women take certain precautions. While no guarantee against rape, they do restore to women a degree of control over their own bodies.

Thinking about one's options (screaming, fighting back, talking, yelling "Fire!") if a rape is attempted is one way to be prepared, and taking some courses in self-defense makes sense as well, if only to bolster a woman's self-confidence and make her appear less vulnerable. But there is no one "right" way to deal with a rapist. Some evidence suggests that resisting may increase the risk of physical injury, and what makes sense in one situation may be pointless in another.

Women living alone should keep entrances well lit and outside doors deadbolted, and should consider using two initials instead of a first name on mailboxes and in telephone listings. Windows should be locked and, whenever possible, covered with iron grids (especially in urban areas or on the first floor of an apartment building). It should be routine to find out the identity of a visitor before opening a door.

Walking in dark parking lots alone, taking strolls through dangerous streets in the wee hours of the morning, and getting into a car before checking the backseat are risky behaviors for all women.

Many colleges provide free shuttle bus services that students can use to avoid walking back to the dormitory alone late at night. Some women always keep keys, Mace, ammonia, or a police whistle ready for use whenever they have to walk alone at night. Others work out commuting arrangements with friends or set up houses of safety where they know they can stop in any time they feel afraid.

Sexual Abuse and Incest

Incest (sexual contact between blood relatives) and sexual abuse of children (sexual contact between an adult and a minor) are considered by most psychiatrists to be acts of violence in which the perpetrator asserts power and control over someone who is defenseless, dependent, and trusting. Occurring in families of every race, educational background, and income level, sexual abuse is most commonly inflicted by fathers, brothers, stepfathers, or stepbrothers, although it is not unknown for mothers to abuse their children sexually (with boys abused by their mothers about twice as often as girls). Fathers who commit incest often have histories of childhood sexual or physical abuse themselves, as well as emotional deprivation, personality disorders, alcohol abuse, and unemployment. Their own low self-esteem and anger often turn them into victimizers of even more helpless family members. The mothers of these abused children also often have a history of being abused as children, and may be victims of domestic abuse, or emotionally unavailable owing to depression or physical illness. Such backgrounds also predispose women to physical abuse of their own children.

One out of every 4 adult women reports having been involved in a nonvoluntary sexual encounter before the age of 18, making women 2 to 4 times more likely than men to have been sexually abused as children. Some investigators estimate that between 15 and 40 percent of all children under 14 in the United States are sexually abused, with 10 percent of that abuse involving incest and the rest involving close friends of the family, teachers, babysitters, or health care professionals—or, much more rarely, strangers.

It is not clear whether the rates of sexual abuse and incest are increasing or whether socialworkers, teachers, and health care professionals are simply looking for them more. Skeptics have argued that leading questions by professionals can make children manufacture incidents that never actually occurred, and undoubtedly there have been some false accusations. Nonetheless, reports of incest and sexual abuse of children are too prevalent to be dismissed as pure fiction.

▸Who is likely to be a victim of sexual abuse or incest?

Although incestuous activity can begin even in infancy, it typically begins with genital fondling or oral-genital stimulation when the child is between 8 and 12 years of age. When the victim reaches puberty, the incest may proceed to sexual intercourse. Being the eldest or the only daughter seems to increase a girl's risk of being sexually abused.

▸What are the aftereffects?

Sexual abuse of young children can lead to scarring and permanent damage to the genitals, rectum, mouth, and throat, and even, in severe cases, death. Abused girls and young women are at high risk for acquiring sexually transmitted diseases, particularly bacterial vaginosis, trichomonas, chlamydia, and AIDS. Because many abused children are prevented from receiving routine medical attention, these problems are often neglected until they become quite serious. After puberty, sexually abused young women risk becoming pregnant.

The long-term effects of childhood sexual abuse and incest generally correlate with the amount of force used and the amount of physical violation involved, as well as with the nature of the relationship and the age difference between the victim and the abuser. Many women with a history of childhood sexual abuse are not aware of any long-term damage, though for others physical and emotional scars can last a lifetime and spark a chain of abuse that may continue for generations.

Women who were sexually abused as children develop high rates of depression, substance abuse, self-destructive behaviors, eating disorders, and multiple personality disorder. Many develop posttraumatic stress disorder as children and live in a state of constant fear and anxiety: some develop learning disabilities or specific delays in speech and motor functions or social skills. Many abused children grow up thinking of themselves as "bad" because a person they loved and trusted treated them so badly. Reflecting on their childhood, many women feel worthless and guilty and persist in the belief that somehow they were at fault for permitting, stimulating, reporting, or not reporting the abuse.

Adult sexual dysfunction is common among victims of childhood sexual abuse, usually involving aversion to sex, distrust of men, and anxiety about intimate relationships. It may also involve difficulty setting sexual boundaries, with the result that some victims of childhood sexual abuse become promiscuous teenagers, prostitutes, or participants in pornography. As many as 4 out of 5 girls who are severely sexually abused will end up as sexually abused women, usually by spouses or other sexual partners. Prone to "revictimization," these women are also more likely than other women to be sexually abused by health care providers.

Even as children, victims may have a hard time knowing the boundaries of intimacy and may develop what psychiatrists call a "disorder of hope" in which they either idealize or despise new acquaintances. The result, in either case, is disappointment and a confirmation of their own helplessness in facing the rest of the world.

Psychosomatic disorders such as conversion disorder (hysteria) and somatization disorder are common in women with a history of childhood incest and sexual abuse. These often manifest themselves as chronic pelvic pain, abdominal pain, or other gastrointestinal problems.

▸ How is sexual abuse evaluated?

Legislation in almost all states requires that any health care professional, teacher, childcare provider, socialworker, or other person who cares for children must report known cases of child abuse. The child is usually put into a protective environment immediately and given a medical and psychological examination as soon as possible so that effective intervention can be taken.

Anyone who becomes aware of someone who sexually abuses a child—including the abuser's private therapist—is also required to report the abuser. Some professionals question the efficacy of this law, feeling that it will keep abusers from seeking help for fear of being reported. Still, the majority opinion is that reporting, handled sensitively, is beneficial for both victim and abuser. The mental health community, which once thought that family therapy could effectively alleviate incest, now believes that the abuser must be arrested before any other therapy can be effective.

▸ How is sexual abuse treated?

Many women who were sexually abused as children have kept this knowledge a deep, dark secret for years. Some do not come to realize the full extent of the crime until they are adults and begin to talk to other women who had more normal childhoods.

Often women find it therapeutic to tell their stories to other women, usually in the form of psychological counseling or support groups for survivors of incest or childhood sexual abuse. Many also seek psychotherapy or other psychiatric attention for specific psychological problems that often result from childhood abuse.

Sexual Behavior
of Women

Sexual Response

Sexual response in humans is as much a function of the mind as of the body. Feelings for the partner, the physical surroundings, fears about pregnancy or AIDS, and personal morals and values about sexuality can all shape a person's sexual satisfaction. There is also considerable individual variation—and variation in the same person at different times—in the types of sexual stimulation that bring pleasure.

For all people, however, the physiology of sexual response is remarkably similar—whether it occurs during masturbation, during heterosexual relations or homosexual relations, in men or in women. In both sexes the physical aspects of sexual response result from increased muscle tension and increased blood circulation in certain parts of the body.

Part of the similarity between the sexes may lie in the embryological origins of the male and female reproductive organs. Both sexes start life with a basically female blueprint, and it is only the production of certain hormones (under genetic direction from the Y chromosome) in male embryos that eventually shapes the penis, testes, scrotum, and seminal vesicles which would otherwise become the vagina, vulva, uterus, ovaries, and fallopian tubes in a female fetus. Because female reproductive organs originate from the same tissue as male organs, some of the female structures correspond to the male ones and respond to the same stimuli. Both the clitoris and the penis, for example, are extremely sensitive to touch (especially at the glans, or tip) and play a central role in sexual pleasure. Both are covered with a hood or foreskin and become engorged with blood during sexual arousal.

▸Phases of human sexual response
During the 1960s the large-scale scientific studies of William Masters and Virginia Johnson divided human sexual response into a four-

phase cycle: excitement, plateau, orgasm, and resolution. Although there is no hard-and-fast barrier between these phases, and sexual fulfillment does not necessarily require experiencing all four of them, this cycle remains the foundation for our understanding of the physical side of human sexual response.

The excitement phase. In the excitement (or arousal) phase, heart rate and blood pressure increase, skin flushes, and nipples become erect in both men and women. The arteries in the genital area become engorged with blood, causing an erection of the penis in men and of the clitoris in women. In women, the labia become engorged with blood and darken in color. Meanwhile, the vaginal lining begins to secrete a lubricating fluid, wetting the vaginal lips.

Various stimuli—physical, mental, emotional, even aesthetic—can trigger the excitement phase. Some women are aroused when their breasts, nipples, thighs, or genitals are touched, while others can be stimulated when less "sexual" areas of the body are caressed or massaged. Fantasies, daydreams, music, colors, thoughts, expressions of affection or desire, or conversation often play a powerful role in arousal.

The plateau phase. This occurs when the muscle contraction and congestion in the pelvis near their peak. In both men and women heart rate and blood pressure increase even more and breathing rate accelerates. In women, the breasts increase in size, the clitoris lifts and retracts under its hood, the vaginal opening swells, and the uterus moves up higher into the pelvis.

The orgasm phase. Also called climax (or, in slang, "coming"), this phase involves sudden rhythmic contractions of the pelvic muscles and genitalia, accompanied by intense feelings of pleasure and a release of tension. In women the contractions occur in the vagina, clitoris, and uterus. In men the contraction of the urethra inside the penis causes ejaculation, the expulsion of seminal fluid (semen). The intensity or pleasurability of an orgasm can vary considerably from one sexual experience to the next.

Claims that stimulation of a sensitive area on the front wall of the vagina called the "G spot," or Grafenberg spot will trigger female orgasm have never been substantiated. Another myth (one that has persisted since it was proposed by Sigmund Freud) is that women can have two different kinds of orgasms: clitoral or vaginal. Clitoral orgasms, which supposedly result from direct clitoral stimulation, were thought to be less mature and less satisfying than vaginal ones, which supposedly occur only during sexual intercourse. Masters and Johnson showed conclusively that, even though they may be produced or perceived differently, from a physiological perspective all orgasms are alike and involve both the clitoris and the vagina.

For many women, having an orgasm (particularly with a partner) is a learned behavior that becomes easier with age and experience. Many women require direct clitoral stimulation to reach orgasm, and most women cannot become adequately excited without foreplay preceding intercourse. Even after penetration women require much more stimulation than do men to reach orgasm. It has been estimated that at least half of heterosexual American women do not regularly have orgasms during sexual intercourse.

Often this situation can be remedied by working together with a partner (sometimes with the help of a sex therapist) to find positions and techniques that are mutually satisfying. This is particularly important if a woman feels inadequate or frustrated because she cannot have an orgasm, or if she has pain or discomfort because of regularly congested pelvic tissues. Despite the women's movement and the explosion of sexuality in American culture, many women still feel shame or guilt about their own sexual needs. Problems with orgasm can sometimes be resolved by learning to acknowledge these sexual needs and communicating them to partners. Often couples need to explore ways of making love that go beyond penis-vagina intercourse.

Many women, however, feel sexually fulfilled (at least some of the time) with the emotional or sensual pleasure that comes from hugging, kissing, being held, or satisfying a partner, and they should not be pressured into trying to have an orgasm. The same is true for women who cannot experience genital sensations because of a disease, disability, or injury but who may be able to receive sexual pleasure from other parts of the body.

The resolution phase. In the last phase of sexual response, the body goes back to its original, unaroused state except that there is a feeling of general well-being. Congestion and erection subside, and respiration, heart rate, and blood pressure return to normal. The time this process takes varies considerably between the sexes. Some (but by no means all) women stay aroused after one orgasm and can continue to have one orgasm after another without passing through the resolution phase. This is called having multiple orgasms. Men generally need a recovery period (called the refractory period) before they can have another orgasm. The refractory period increases with age and can range in any individual from a few minutes to half a day.

Sexual Preference

Not so long ago anyone whose sexual preference was other than purely heterosexual—that is, anyone who was ever attracted to a member of the same sex—was universally considered deviant. Homosexuality was believed to be a form of disease (mental or physical) from which people could and should be cured. In 1973, however, the American Psychiatric Association (APA) declared that preference for a person of one's own sex is neither a psychiatric disorder nor a disease but merely one of several normal forms of sexual expression. Although there is still considerable debate about whether sexual preference is determined primarily by culture or primarily by biology (which can include prenatal development as well as genetic endowment), very few authorities still believe that people consciously choose to be homosexual or heterosexual.

Newer research on sexual behavior and feelings indicates that a person's sexual preference is not as clear-cut as was once believed. Instead, most researchers today regard sexual preference as falling somewhere along a continuum (first proposed by the sex researcher Alfred Kinsey) ranging from exclusive heterosexuality to exclusive homosexuality. Most people fall somewhere between the two extremes of the continuum, usually significantly closer to one end or the other. People who are primarily attracted to members of the other sex are called heterosexuals, and those primarily attracted to members of the same sex (an estimated 10 percent of the U.S. population) are called homosexuals (or, in the case of women, lesbians). The many people whose sexual preference is closer to the middle of the continuum and who feel attracted to both men and women (though not necessarily to the same degree) are known as bisexuals.

Just where a person falls on this sexual preference continuum is not always immediately obvious. Not only do many teenagers experiment with both heterosexual and homosexual behavior before learning what is most natural to them, but also women in particular (many of them married, with children) are apt to discover a homosexual leaning well into life, only when they have enough time, confidence, and experience for self-awareness. Other women know they have homosexual feelings at an early age but do not choose to act on these feelings until much later.

Various studies suggest that as many as 20 percent of all American women have had some kind of intimate relationship with another woman, either exclusively or in addition to relationships with men. These numbers would be much higher if they included women who are attracted to other women but never act on (or even acknowledge) these feelings. Increasing awareness about, and acceptance of, homosexuality among the American public (as reflected in laws upholding basic rights regardless of sexual orientation) has gone a long way toward encouraging more and more homosexuals of both sexes to come out of the closet. Even so, there is still a pervasive taboo about homosexuality, which leads to various forms of discrimination—including difficulties adopting or gaining custody of children and getting or keeping jobs, particularly jobs involving children. Homosexuals often find themselves ridiculed, chastised, or ostracized by peers and family members—and this treatment results in considerable stress, feelings of loneliness, isolation, depression, and low self-esteem.

Lesbians are more likely than women in the general population to attempt suicide and to have problems with alcohol and substance abuse. These facts suggest a higher rate of depression (often untreated) among this group of women. Because the homosexual community provides some support against homophobia, for many lesbians homosexuality becomes a matter of personal identity and lifestyle as well as a sexual preference.

Sexual Dysfunction

The exact incidence of sexual dysfunction in the general population is not known, but a recent survey ranked sexual difficulties fourth among the top problems facing heterosexual American couples, after rapid social change, domestic abuse, and money.

There are three basic types of sexual dysfunction. The first type, disorders of desire, takes the form of inadequate sexual desire (libido) in both sexes. The second type, disorders of excitement (or arousal), involve insufficient vaginal lubrication (wetness) in women and, in men, impotence (failure to attain or maintain an erection through the completion of the sexual act). Some women may also experience vaginismus, a disorder in which the muscles in the entrance to the vagina contract involuntarily, making intercourse difficult and painful, if not impossible. The third type of sexual dysfunction, disorders of orgasm, include difficulty achieving orgasm, and, in men, premature ejaculation (orgasm that occurs before the man wishes it to occur).

These disorders often happen together, and problems in one partner can affect the other. Lack of sexual desire in a heterosexual woman, for example, may ultimately affect her partner's ability to achieve an erection. Similarly, a man who experiences premature ejaculation or who does not engage in adequate foreplay may make orgasm difficult or impossible for his partner.

A whole host of factors, both physical and psychological, may underlie these problems. Male sexual dysfunctions (such as impotence) once thought to be purely psychological have now been shown in many cases to have a physiological basis. Far less is known about the physiological roots of female sexual dysfunction, but many diseases, disabilities, and surgical procedures (as well as premenstrual syndrome) have been linked to sexual problems in women; in addition, various medications can also significantly alter sexual functioning (see charts).

Sexual pleasure in humans is as much a product of the mind as the body. Depression, anger, anxiety, and fear can interfere with a person's ability to enjoy sexual activity. Many women find that their sexual response is inextricably linked to other, nonsexual feelings they have for their partner. Mundane squabbles, lack of communication, basic incompatibility, arguments over money, and marital infidelity all impinge on sexual response. A man or woman exhausted from stress at work or other responsibilities may simply have no energy left to engage in the flirtation or seduction behavior necessary for enjoyable sex.

Sometimes sexual dysfunction can be traced to a lack of information about sexuality and sexual response—such as not knowing the importance of adequate foreplay or the fact that females generally require much more time than males to reach orgasm. Even women aware of these things may feel uncomfortable expressing their needs to their partner. Other women, afraid of feeling vulnerable, may have problems "letting go" or losing control. They may also worry about what their partner is thinking about them or fear that they are not doing the right thing to give and experience pleasure.

Growing up in a family with negative attitudes about sex can interfere with a woman's enjoyment of her sexuality, as can earlier traumatic sexual experiences such as rape or incest, which may lead a woman to equate sex with impropriety, danger, or pain.

▸ Disorders of desire

Sex drive ebbs and flows in the course of a relationship, and it is common for one partner to desire sex more often than another. Although these problems may be temporarily troublesome and require better communication, they are not considered dysfunctions per se. In contrast, women whose sexual desire is low (a condition called hypoactive sexual desire disorder or, more simply, low libido) persistently have little or no interest in sex and rarely if ever have sexual fantasies. (The term frigidity, formerly used to describe this disorder, has been discarded because of its vague meaning and derogatory connotations.) Low libido usually goes hand in hand with disorders of arousal and orgasm, but some women can go on to experience orgasm despite having little desire for sexual intercourse. About half the people who see doctors about sexual disorders say that lack of desire is their main problem (most people who complain of this are men).

Physical health, attractiveness of the partner, sensory stimulation,

Disorders and surgeries that can affect sexual response in women

Endocrine problems	Associated sexual dysfunction
Diabetes	Reduced vaginal lubrication; vaginal infections
Thyroid, adrenal, or pituitary gland disorders	Reduced vaginal lubrication

Vascular problems	
Sickle cell anemia	Decreased arousal and orgasm
Heart disorders such as heart attack or angina	Fear of death leading to reduced frequency of sexual activity

Neurologic problems	
Spinal cord damage or multiple sclerosis	Decreased arousal, orgasm, and vaginal lubrication

Gynecologic problems	
Vaginitis, pelvic inflammatory disease (PID), or endometriosis	Vaginismus; pain during sexual intercourse
Prolapsed uterus or uterine fibroids	Decreased arousal and desire

Kidney problems	
Kidney failure (using dialysis)	Decreased arousal and desire; electrolyte and hormone imbalance

Musculoskeletal problems	
Arthritis	Chronic pain; limited motion
Sjögren syndrome	Decreased lubrication

Surgical procedures	
Oophorectomy or episiotomy	Decreased estrogens and lubrication; tightness of vaginal opening
Mastectomy or colostomy	Loss of self-esteem and fears of discomfort that may interfere with any phase of sexual function

thoughts, and emotions all play a role in creating sexual desire. Whereas some women have never had any interest in sex, for others a reduced sex drive is a temporary response to an alteration in lifestyle, health, or relationships. Lifestyle changes after the birth of a child, for example, may diminish a woman's sex drive. After full days tending children or balancing childcare and job-related duties, a new mother may find herself uninterested in sex with a partner she no longer has much of a relationship with outside of the bedroom. Sexual interest is also bound to decline in a woman who believes that her partner does not listen to her or appreciate her, who resents her partner's lack of help with housework, childcare, cooking, and shopping, or who feels that her partner does not make enough effort to please her sexually.

Low libido is also a characteristic symptom of depression and may occur as a side effect of numerous medications. It can be a logical consequence of painful intercourse, which is common in many gynecological infections and disorders. In some older women painful intercourse can result from thinning vaginal walls (vaginal atrophy) and inadequate natural lubrication, and this may reduce the desire for sex, as may the hormonal changes of menopause.

Because so many different factors are involved, a disorder of desire can be difficult to treat in women. Simply having more positive sexual experiences can help. Other women find that their libido revives after they are treated for some underlying illness or after they switch medications or discontinue the one that was causing their symptoms. If a woman has a history of menstrual irregularity or other physical disorders, the doctor may want to check levels of various hormones in the blood and treat any underlying imbalances.

If the cause of low libido appears to be nonphysical, certain exercises advocated by sex therapists often help. These include sensate focus exercises—a series of "pleasuring" techniques developed by the sex therapists William Masters and Virginia Johnson in the 1960s to enhance enjoyment without any pressure to perform in some predetermined way. Many therapists also encourage the use of erotic materials, as well as training women to masturbate while fantasizing so that they can become aware of conditions necessary for a positive sexual experience. Women who have a life history of

Medications that can affect sexual response in women

Antihypertensives	**Side effect**
Methyldopa, reserpine, clonidine, propranolol, or spironolactone	Decreased libido; difficulty having orgasms
Anticholinergics	
Propantheline or methantheline	Decreased lubrication
Hormones	
Estrogen, progesterone, or steroids	Decreased libido (sometimes)
Androgens	Increased libido
Psychotropics	
Sedatives, such as alcohol or barbiturates	Various sexual problems at high doses
Antianxiety medications, such as diazepam and alprazolam	Difficulty having orgasms
Antipsychotics, such as thioridazine	Difficulty having orgasms
Antidepressants, including	Difficulty having orgasms
MAOIs, such as phenelzine	
Tricyclics, such as imipramine, clomipramine	
SSRIs, such as Prozac (fluoxetine), Zoloft (sertraline), and Paxil (paroxetine)	
Trazodone	Increased libido (sometimes)
Lithium	Decreased libido
Opiates	
Morphine, codeine, methadone	Decreased libido; difficulty having orgasms
Miscellaneous	
Phenytoin, indomethacin, clofibrate, cimetidine, or carbamazine	Decreased libido

low libido may need further counseling to see if they may have a deeper aversion to pleasure in general.

Women with the rarer but still fairly common condition called sexual aversion disorder are so repulsed by the idea of sex that they avoid genital sexual contact with a partner. Often people with this disorder have phobias, or deep-seated fears, about sexual activity or even the thought of sexual activity. Typically people with this disorder have intercourse only once or twice a year, but they often have a fairly natural sexual response once they get past their initial dread and anxiety. Men with sexual aversion disorder tend to have it from an early age, while women more frequently develop it after years of normal sexual desires.

About a quarter of people with sexual phobias and aversions also have panic disorder. When sexual aversion disorder is related to panic attacks, it is relatively easy to treat by taking antipanic medications such as tricyclic antidepressants (imipramine) or benzodiazepines (alprazolam) for about 3 or 4 months. Otherwise, the treatment is similar to that for hypoactive sexual desire.

▶ Disorders of excitement

During sexual excitation the vaginal lining secretes a lubricating fluid and the inner lips and clitoris become engorged with blood. When women have problems attaining or maintaining this response through the completion of sexual activity, they are said to have excitement phase disorder. Many women with this disorder also have problems with sexual desire and feel pain during intercourse.

Arousal problems can occur for mundane reasons. Sexually inexperienced women, for example, may for the first few times focus more on how they perform than on how they feel. Similarly, women who are afraid of becoming pregnant at certain times of the month may have problems with arousal, as may women who attempt intercourse without adequate foreplay or stimulation.

Often hormonal deficiencies account for these symptoms. In women nearing or past menopause, for example, a deficiency of estrogen can dry the lining of the vagina. Vaginal lubrication also tends to be sparser during menstruation and for the first few days afterwards, as well as after childbirth and during breastfeeding. If the excitement phase disorder is due to a deficiency of estrogen, it can be easily treated by intermittently applying topical estrogen cream to the vagina and by using water-based lubricants such as K-Y Jelly, Transi-Lube, or Replens. (Petroleum jellies such as Vaseline should be avoided, since they do not dissolve in the vagina and can foster bacterial growth.)

More frequently, however, some psychological problem, including depression or stress, underlies the disorder. Women who feel longstanding anger or hostility toward their partner may have problems becoming aroused. For these women most doctors advise psychotherapy or marital therapy to help alleviate the underlying problem.

▸ Disorders of orgasm

That women often "fake" orgasms has become a cliché. This is probably because having an orgasm is a difficult feat for many women. Some of the problem lies in unrealistic expectations. The belief that the only "real" orgasms occur during sexual intercourse, that simultaneous orgasm with a partner is essential to sexual fulfillment, or even that having an orgasm every time is necessary for sexual satisfaction can contribute to a woman's feelings of inadequacy.

Some women cannot relax because of distrust and fear of vulnerability, while others feel guilty about sexual pleasure and do not allow themselves to experience it. Any kind of discord in the relationship can also lead to difficulties with orgasm.

But much of the problem with orgasm can be traced to physiological factors. Most women require much more foreplay and stimulation than do most men before reaching orgasm. And at least 30 to 40 percent of women require direct clitoral stimulation (manual or oral) and are unable to have an orgasm with intercourse alone. This is perfectly normal, but unless a woman learns to communicate her needs to her partner and the couple tries to modify their sexual activity to fit them, orgasmic problems are almost inevitable.

Between 5 and 8 percent of women are unable to achieve orgasm during intercourse, even with direct clitoral stimulation. Some women can have orgasms during masturbation but not with a partner, while others do not have orgasms under any circumstances. When a woman cannot have an orgasm with a partner, despite normal desire and excitement phases, she is said to have orgasmic dysfunction.

For some women the solution to this problem is a matter of

practice and experience. For others, a variety of specific exercises and techniques have been highly successful. For women who have never had an orgasm, a doctor or sex therapist will usually provide education about female sexual response and then encourage self-exploration, including masturbation and use of fantasy material. In addition, practicing Kegel vaginal exercises can help develop muscles in the vagina called the pubococcygeus muscles, which are involved in orgasm. Through these techniques about 90 percent of women being treated eventually achieve orgasm.

Women who have trouble having orgasms with a partner are given sensate focus exercises to help discover or rediscover what is pleasurable. These usually begin with nongenital stimulation (with intercourse and orgasms prohibited) to take away performance pressure. If a woman wants to experience orgasm during intercourse, many sex therapists advocate the "bridge technique," in which the clitoris is stimulated manually or with a vibrator while the penis is inserted into the vagina. Other couples find it helpful to have sex in a "back protected" position (in which the partner sits with the woman between the partner's legs and her back against the partner's chest). This allows the woman to control stimulation without unnecessary self-consciousness. Heterosexual couples are also encouraged to explore pelvic thrusting in a nondemanding way, beginning with female superior position, followed by a lateral (side-by-side) position which allows both partners to move freely.

Success of these techniques depends greatly on the nature of the couple's relationship. About 30 to 50 percent of women who try these techniques eventually learn to have regular orgasms during intercourse. About 70 to 80 percent will be able to experience orgasm with a partner, but not necessarily during intercourse.

▸ Pain during sexual intercourse

When a woman frequently experiences vaginal pain before, during, or after sexual intercourse, the condition is called dyspareunia. Approximately 1 in 5 women may suffer from this disorder at any given time, and many more experience it at some point in their lives. Dyspareunia results when there is not enough lubrication in the vaginal walls to relieve friction between the penis and vagina. It can occur in any woman who has intercourse without adequate stimulation, as well as in women with disorders of desire or excitement, or who are anxious about their sexual performance. Dyspareunia can initiate a vicious cycle in which fear and anticipation of pain interfere with arousal and the natural lubrication that it would otherwise produce.

When the pain is felt deep inside the vagina, there may be an underlying disorder of the pelvic organs. These disorders include endometriosis, pelvic inflammatory disease (PID), adhesions, ovarian cancer, ovarian cysts, or tears in the ligaments that support the uterus. Occasionally deep vaginal pain may occur when the penis hits the cervix (the opening to the uterus) during thrusting. This can often be alleviated by changing positions.

Vaginismus is a relatively rare form of sexual pain disorder in which muscles in the outer third of the vagina (pubococcygeus muscles) involuntary contract to prevent penetration, making sexual intercourse impossible, difficult, or painful. Many unconsummated marriages of long duration can be attributed to vaginismus in the woman. Partners of women with vaginismus can develop impotence as well.

Vaginismus seems to be a way for the body to avoid sexual contact. It is particularly common in women who experienced sexual trauma such as rape.

▸ Sadomasochism

Sadomasochism is a highly controversial form of sexual expression in which sexual excitement is enhanced through an unequal power relationship between the partners. It is a combination of sadistic behavior in one partner (inflicting pain on another person to heighten one's sexual pleasure) and masochistic behavior in the other (experiencing pain, suffering, or humiliation to heighten one's sexual pleasure). S/M often involves a fantasy situation in which each partner takes on a role. One partner may be the teacher while the other is the student, for example, or one may be the master while the other is the slave. Ideally, this playacting comes to a stop when either partner wants it to.

Defenders of sadomasochism argue that S/M is a healthy form of sexual expression because it allows consenting partners to express the power issues that are a natural, if hidden, part of sexuality. Moreover, particularly in homosexual relationships, the roles can be reversed at will, allowing each partner an opportunity to be dominant and subordinate. But many critics, including feminist critics of mainstream sexuality, have expressed concern about the practice of S/M. They argue that, in heterosexuals, this behavior reinforces traditional male-female relationships and, in all relationships, it may encourage or mask dangerous situations such as domestic abuse or rape.

If a woman involved in an S/M relationship believes her partner may suffer from true sexual sadism, she should seek help from her clinician or from a battered women's shelter. Sexual sadism is a kind of paraphilia, that is, a gross impairment of a person's ability to engage in affectionate sexual activity. Paraphilias occur almost exclusively in men. In contrast to most rapists, who are motivated more by violent than by sexual impulses, sexual sadists derive sexual excitement and pleasure from brutally hurting their partners. Many people fantasize about inflicting pain, but sexual sadists actually enact their fantasies and sometimes inflict extensive or mortal injuries. Long-term psychotherapy can sometimes help people with this problem.

▸ How is sexual dysfunction treated?

Some sexual problems can be worked through with the help of good books and a caring partner, whereas others might call for professional help. For many women, turning to friends or women's support groups may provide valuable ways of dealing with sexual dysfunction. This is particularly true for lesbians or women with disabilities, who tend to have trouble finding health care professionals attuned to their particular problems. Many popular books on the subject of sexuality offer valuable suggestions for overcoming sexual dysfunction.

Women who suspect that they may have more serious physical, psychological, or marital problems may want to seek help from a health care provider trained in sex counseling or from a sex therapist. If there is an underlying physical problem, the solution involves treating that problem or changing a medication. Most problems will entail additional changes, however, and these often require the cooperation of both partners.

The techniques of sex therapy, a relatively new form of short-term psychotherapy which emphasizes behavioral changes in contrast to elucidating underlying causes of a problem, have helped some couples. A sex therapist (or doctor trained in sex therapy) usually takes a history of the woman or the couple, provides information about sexual anatomy and response, and then offers specific suggestions and exercises that both partners can attempt at home to try to heighten sexual pleasure. Sex therapists emphasize increasing communication between partners, decreasing performance anxiety by changing the goal of the sexual activity from emphasis on orgasm toward feeling good, and encouraging sexual experimentation.

Although sex therapy is frequently effective—especially in treating disorders of excitement and orgasm—some couples may need more intensive psychotherapy or couples counseling as well. This is particularly true for people with inadequate sexual desire, since this dysfunction tends to stem from more complex (and often cerebral) factors and cannot usually be remedied with short-term behavioral techniques.

Because anyone can hang up a shingle as a sex therapist, finding a competent and reputable one can be a challenge. Sex therapy is rarely effective unless it is practiced by a person also trained in the more broadly based couples and family therapy, and who is also capable of assessing and treating individual psychological problems that may have nothing to do with sexual dysfunction per se. Anyone seeking a sex therapist should be wary of therapists who suggest genital surgery as the solution to sexual dysfunction. And they should avoid any so-called sex therapist who asks them to engage in sexual exercises in the office or to observe sexual activities there or who offers to serve as a "sex surrogate." A good source of certified sex therapists is the national register put out by the American Association of Sex Education Counselors and Therapists.

Women with vaginismus can be helped further with behavioral modification techniques. Usually a doctor will recommend a series of desensitization exercises, to be practiced at home, in which the vaginal muscles are gradually trained to accept penetration. First the woman is encouraged to insert a finger into the vagina, then several. Vaginal dilators of graduated sizes are usually the next step in training the vaginal muscles to relax. Eventually she will be encouraged to attempt intercourse in a female-superior position, using her partner's erect penis, coated with extra vaginal lubricant, as a dilator. In some cases psychotherapy or hypnosis may also be helpful.

Taking Control

Stress

Strictly speaking, stress is any kind of force or pressure. This pressure can be physical, such as the stress of exercise or the stress of a debilitating disease, as well as emotional or situational, such as the stress of a high-pressure, low-freedom job. Today the term stress is loosely applied to virtually any event or situation that can evoke frustration, anger, or anxiety.

Whatever its source, true stress triggers a characteristic physiological response known as the fight-or-flight response (also called physiological stress). In this response the brain sends signals to the adrenal glands which lead them to secrete the "stress hormones" epinephrine and norepinephrine. These hormones cause muscles to tense, heart rate and blood pressure to increase, and breathing to accelerate. The fight-or-flight response originally evolved to prepare animals to respond to danger, and in this sense stress was a very positive factor that helped preserve and protect life.

Many forms of stress are positive. The stress triggered by regular exercise, for example, can be invigorating, as can the mental stress posed by a challenging work or school assignment. The same stress that may frustrate one person may motivate or relax another. We all know people who are tense and miserable on the beach, for example, but who appear to thrive when tackling a project at work. Nevertheless, for many people modern life is fraught with all sorts of frustrations and threats to which the only acceptable response is internalized misery. In the case of women the sources of stress may be boring and low-paying jobs, sexual discrimination or harassment, sexual and domestic abuse, lack of empathy from a partner, the strain of balancing work and family life, or (sometimes) the boredom and frustration of staying home with children while partners and neighbors develop stimulating careers. The result is often prolonged negative stress.

Social readjustment rating scale

Life event	Life-change units
Death of one's spouse	100
Divorce	73
Marital separation	65
Jail term	63
Death of a close family member	63
Personal injury or illness	53
Marriage	50
Being fired	47
Marital reconciliation	45
Retirement	45
Health change in a family member	44
Pregnancy	40
Sex difficulties	39
Gain of a new family member	39
Business readjustment	39
Change in one's financial state	38
Death of a close friend	37
Change to a different line of work	36
More arguments with one's spouse	35
Mortgage over $10,000*	31
Foreclosure of a mortgage or loan	30
Change in responsibilities at work	29
Son or daughter leaving home	29
Trouble with in-laws	29
Outstanding achievement	28

Life event	Life-change units
Spouse beginning or stopping work	26
Beginning or ending school	26
Change in living conditions	25
Revision of personal habits	24
Trouble with one's boss	23
Change in work hours or conditions	20
Change in residence	20
Change in schools	20
Change in recreation	19
Change in church activities	19
Change in social activities	18
Mortgage or loan under $10,000*	17
Change in sleeping habits	16
Change in family get-togethers	15
Change in eating habits	15
Vacation	13
Christmas	12
Minor violations of the law	11

The SRRS, developed by Holmes and Rahe in 1967, assigned "life-change units" to several dozen stressful events and linked the number to risk for medical problems.

*Note that the mortgage sum of $10,000 reflects economic realities of over 20 years ago. $100,000 might be closer to the realities of today, in many parts of the United States.

Classic research on the impact of negative *and* positive life events on health has produced a scale of life stressors (see chart). These studies show that positive events (such as getting married or having a baby) as well as negative ones (death of a spouse, divorce, job loss) temporarily increase the chance of becoming physically ill.

Psychologists have tried to develop strict definitions for "stress" and "anxiety" and other behavioral terms in order to allow scientific study of their effect on emotional health and physical well-being. But most of the studies on these risk factors so far have used subtly different definitions; thus, it is hard to compare results. Furthermore, many studies rely on self-ratings, asking subjects questions such as "Do you feel upset when . . . ?" or "Do you find this stressful?" Yet the way people rate their own emotions is subjective: what one woman calls anxious, another might call normal. This lack of objective measurements makes it hard to compare one subject with the next, much less compare studies.

Finally, the theories relating behavior and emotions to physical health sound just a little too pat. Society always has a tendency to blame the victim when there is no obvious physical explanation for a problem, and the psychosocial-behavioral findings sound judgmental: they imply that people would not have heart disease or other health problems if they were not so obsessed with their work, anxious, easily upset, or (fill in the blank). If people just changed their behavior, they would not be sick. Thus, having a stress-related illness is not the same as being inadvertently exposed to a bacterium or hit by a car. There is always a subtle implication that we are more to blame for our behavioral and attitudinal failings than our physical ones, perhaps because people assume that these basic emotions are more easily controlled.

Even so, the accumulation of evidence implicating stress as a risk factor in physical health cannot be denied. Although recent evidence suggests that the role of emotions and behaviors in disease is probably more complex than previously believed, it is hard to dismiss the many studies suggesting that people who experience anxiety, depression, neuroticism, sleep disturbances, emotional drain, or a tendency to express emotional problems as bodily complaints may be more prone to various physical diseases and disorders than the general population.

▸ Who is likely to develop high levels of stress?

The modern woman is said to be drowning in a sea of stress. In addition to the traditional sources of stress—such as the demands of young children and aging parents—many women today also face considerable stress in the workplace. Since the late 1960s, 300 hours of work—including time spent at work as well as time spent caring for a household—have been added to a working woman's annual schedule. "Working moms" are the major breadwinner in many two-parent families, and the only breadwinner in the vast majority of single-parent families. Although both men and women often feel stressed from repetitive, unstimulating work, stress for women is compounded by pay inequity (women's pay is still on average only 71 percent that of men with comparable training and responsibilities), the lack of adequate health insurance and other benefits (especially in parts of the service sector where the majority of women work), a "glass ceiling" and "mommy track" that prevent women from rising to positions of authority as often or as rapidly as men with comparable abilities, and, above all else, the difficulty of balancing work and family responsibilities.

A report by the U.S. Department of Labor has revealed that working women rank stress as their greatest everyday problem. The largest number of complaints came from women in their 40s who had professional and managerial jobs, and from single mothers who said that their biggest problem is balancing family and work, including finding affordable childcare.

Interpersonal conflict seems to be particularly stressful to women, whereas competition and intellectual challenge are more stressful to men. Studies have shown that competitive challenges lead to greater than average elevations in blood pressure—even during sleep—in men. Such findings suggest that difficult work permanently damages the circulatory system (or, alternatively, that men with high blood pressure tend to choose high-pressure jobs). But when it comes to women, the pressures of work seem much less likely to affect blood pressure. The only exceptions are women in top management jobs.

What does seem to send women's blood pressure soaring are interpersonal conflicts and strains at home, especially problems with partners and children. These findings make things look particularly bleak for young women in upper management who go home to children and other family responsibilities. Men tend to relax after leaving a high-pressure job, but women with equivalent jobs often get no relief. This unremitting stress of the "second shift" is what ultimately sends many women around the bend, emotionally and, eventually, physically.

During their reproductive years, these young women may have a built-in buffer against the physical effects of stress because of the protective effects of estrogen—particularly its effect on serum cholesterol levels. Although LDL cholesterol levels (which have been linked to heart attack risk) were higher in women managers, protective HDL levels also remained high in all women, regardless of the nature of their job or their personality type.

▸ How can women alleviate stress?

Some women may handle the stress in their lives better than men because they are better able to identify and deal with it. By venting their frustrations with friends or even allowing themselves a good cry, women may be dispelling some of the most toxic effects of stress. Aware that their lives are stressful, women may purposefully adopt a healthier lifestyle, perhaps choosing foods more carefully, losing weight, cutting out cigarettes, getting enough sleep, or embarking on an exercise plan—which often helps vent frustration in and of itself.

Women who feel overwhelmed by stress may want to try adopting some of these stress-resistant strategies (see chart). Delineating specific sources of stress, prioritizing demands, and learning to find satisfaction in less frustrating areas of life can work wonders. Establishing a stable daily routine, actively seeking social support, and believing in one's personal ability to solve problems can help some women better manage stress. For extremely compulsive women, stress can be reduced by accepting the necessity, sometimes, of a temporary disruption in one's daily routine, or realizing that one cannot solve all of one's problems at the same time.

Relaxation exercises can often undo some of the stresses of everyday life. Transcendental meditation and yoga, practiced over many months or years, have been credited with lowering elevated blood pressure and with making people feel less anxious and out of con-

Stress-reducing techniques

Change your environment

Reduce external stress such as noise and pollution
Reduce stimulation at home when possible
Reduce stimulation at work when possible
Reduce threats to your physical safety

Change your behavior

Eat a balanced diet
Get enough sleep
Get adequate exercise
Learn relaxation techniques or meditation
Cut back on alcohol and caffeine consumption
Reduce exposure to situations that involve conflict
Take a time-management course
Undergo hypnosis

Develop a new attitude

Set limits for yourself and others
Become more aware of other options
Become more aware of what you are feeling
Be more willing to express what you are feeling
Become more confident about your own perceptions
Become more aware of the possibility of internal change

trol, as has hypnosis (see Alternative Therapies). In some situations becoming more assertive can alleviate stress: it may be helpful to speak up about job frustrations, or to investigate a company's grievance procedures. Taking a course in time management or in meditation techniques has given many women relief during periods of unusual stress.

Premenstrual Syndrome

Many clinicians define premenstrual syndrome as some combination of physical, mood, or behavioral changes which occur consistently and predictably before or during each menstrual period and which are severe enough to interfere with some aspects of a woman's life. A woman who starts feeling weepy, "headachy," and bloated about 5 to 15 days before her period is due each month may be said to have PMS. The same is true for a normally calm woman who becomes so overwhelmed by feelings of anger in the days before her period that she screams at her children and cannot concentrate on her work. Having just a few isolated symptoms, such as a craving for chocolate, moodiness, or cramps, before or at the beginning of menstruation is not the same as having premenstrual syndrome, unless these symptoms are severe enough to interfere with normal activity.

Given the enormous hormonal changes associated with the menstrual cycle, it is no wonder that many women experience changes in physical functioning, mood, or behavior over the course of the month. Most women probably go through at least some kind of noticeable physical or psychological changes during the week before menstruation begins. What is more mysterious is why these changes become disabling in some women. There do not seem to be differences in daily levels of various hormones in women with and without PMS. There does seem to be some evidence that changes in ovarian hormones may modify circadian rhythms (the body's precisely timed physiological response to light-dark cycles over 24 hours), decrease sensitivity to endorphins (the body's natural pain-killers), or decrease the levels of the neurotransmitter serotonin in the brain (which can lead to irritability and depression). But precisely how or why is still unclear. It may also turn out that there is more than one form of PMS, each associated with a different underlying mechanism.

▸ Who is likely to develop PMS?

Many clinicians, and many more women, have observed anecdotally that PMS symptoms worsen for some women as they approach menopause. There has been so little well-designed research in this area, however, that these observations have not yet been proven conclusively. The most serious cases of PMS, affecting 1 to 5 percent of all women, seem to occur most often in women who are between the ages of 26 and 35, who have cycle lengths of 25 to 28 days, and who report having experienced stressful life events in the preceding year. Other factors associated with severe PMS are a personal or family history of depression; a history of migraine headaches or postpartum depression; having several children; and a higher than average intake of alcohol or chocolate.

Some other psychiatric disorders are a risk factor for PMS. Two thirds of women who suffer from depression also have premenstrual syndrome, and 45 to 70 percent of women with PMS have a past history of depression. About a third of women with PMS who also have children have a history of mild to severe postpartum depression, which is twice the rate in the normal population. If a woman has an underlying psychiatric illness, chances are these symptoms will worsen during the premenstrual phase of her monthly cycle. For example, many women who have panic attacks find that the frequency of attacks increases in the premenstrual phase. The rate of PMS in women with personality disorders does not seem to be any higher than in the general population of women.

▸ What are the symptoms?

Like seasonal affective disorder and postpartum psychiatric disorders (see above), PMS is primarily characterized by the timing of symptoms. There are literally hundreds of symptoms that may occur in PMS, but what makes them distinctive is that they are severe enough to disrupt daily activity and that they begin during the last 5 to 15 days of each menstrual cycle and stop during menstruation. Among the most frequent symptoms of PMS are acne, anger, anxiety, appetite changes, bloating, breast pain, depression, difficulty concentrating, fatigue, headaches, joint swelling, mood swings, nausea, nervousness, pelvic pain, sleep disorders, sweating, vomiting, and weight gain.

The American Psychiatric Association also has specific diagnostic criteria for what it has termed premenstrual dysphoric disorder, which may or may not be the same as PMS. The symptoms of this disorder largely involve the mood changes (as opposed to the physical symptoms) that may occur cyclically in women. To be diagnosed as having this disorder a woman must have at least 5 of the following symptoms: mood swings, anger or irritability, anxiety or tension, depressed mood, decreased interest in usual activities, fatigue, difficulty concentrating, increase or decrease in appetite, sleep disturbance, and physical symptoms such as breast pain, bloating, or headaches. These symptoms must occur cyclically and during most of the woman's menstrual cycles, and they must be serious enough to interfere with activities.

▸ How is the condition evaluated?

In evaluating premenstrual syndrome, a clinician will take a careful history that includes information about the nature, timing, and severity of the symptoms. Before an effective treatment plan can be made, the clinician will need to understand the woman's living situation, diet, and exercise habits, and determine if the woman or her family has any psychiatric problems or history of alcohol or substance abuse.

A thorough physical and pelvic examination, and possibly certain laboratory tests as well, will be done to see if there are any underlying systemic disorders such as hypothyroidism or anemia which may mimic PMS or if there are any anatomical disorders such as endometriosis or uterine fibroids which may be contributing to pelvic pain.

The clinician will also ask the woman to record her symptoms on a daily basis for at least two complete menstrual cycles (see chart). This is the best way to see just how—and if—symptoms are linked to the menstrual cycle.

▸ How is PMS treated?

Because of the variety of symptoms found in PMS, there is no one, universally effective treatment. Among the many different approaches are changes in lifestyle; support groups and other stress management techniques; vitamin supplements; and drugs aimed at relieving specific symptoms or groups of symptoms. With information about PMS treatments still so limited, it remains difficult to predict which women will respond to which therapies. Thus, treating PMS often requires trial and error, and it may take several months, even a year, to arrive at the optimal treatment.

Usually the first line of attack involves modifying diet and exercise habits. Many women find that eliminating caffeine, alcohol, and sugary foods, eating frequent small meals, and ensuring adequate protein and complex carbohydrate intake help control PMS symptoms. Regular aerobic exercise for 20 to 45 minutes a day at least 3 times a week seems to benefit some women with PMS. Others find that eating carbohydrate-rich meals during the evenings of the second half of the menstrual cycle also helps, possibly because this diet may raise levels of the neurotransmitter serotonin (which, when low, has been linked to depression). One randomized trial suggested that a strict low-fat diet (less than 15 percent of calories from fat) reduces premenstrual breast pain.

Joining a support group, especially one led by a leader trained in group psychotherapy, can be helpful. Often members of the group keep daily records of their symptoms and discuss any relationship they may have with the menstrual cycle, as well as with any changes made in diet or exercise habits. Support groups can provide new ideas about effective relaxation and stress management strategies and generate discussion about other lifestyle changes that may ease symptoms. The peer support available in these groups can make it easier to implement these changes. And simply meeting other women who have similar symptoms can make a woman with PMS feel less alone and help affirm that her condition is not "all in her head."

Admittedly, the rationale for the diet, exercise, and stress management approaches comes more from trial and error than from randomized clinical trials (the gold standard in scientific studies). Still, they are certainly worth trying, given the minimal risk and cost involved, as well as the fact that many women have found them effective.

If symptoms persist, another approach may be to try various vitamin or mineral supplements. Among the most promising of these are calcium (1,000 mg each day), magnesium (200 mg taken during the last half of the cycle), vitamin B_6 (50 to 200 mg each day), and vitamin E (150 to 400 IU each day). These recommendations are based on only a handful of studies and may not work for all women.

Monthly record of premenstrual experiences

Cycle day 1 is the day that bleeding starts. Enter the dates of the cycle (for example, 3/15) in the second row. Record your daily weight (taken first thing in the morning, no clothing) in the third row. Then, throughout the cycle, indicate the severity of any symptoms, using 0 (not present), 1 (noticeable but not troublesome), 2 (interferes with normal activities), or 3 (intolerable). Use these numbers to record bleeding, in the fourth row.

Cycle day	1	2	3	4	5	6	7	8	9	10	11	12	13	14	15	16	17	18	19	20	21	22	23	24	25	26	27	28	29	30	31
Date																															
Weight																															
Bleeding																															
Acne																															
Bloatedness																															
Breast tenderness																															
Dizziness																															
Fatigue																															
Headache																															

	Hot flashes	Nausea	Diarrhea	Constipation	Palpitations	Swelling	Angry outbursts	Anxiety	Difficulty concentrating	Crying easily	Depression	Food cravings	Forgetfulness	Mood swings	Overly sensitive	Wish to be alone

Still, at least when it comes to vitamin B_6, there seems to be a verifiable mechanism for action. This vitamin plays a role in the metabolism of serotonin, and there are some studies showing that it can alleviate the depression associated with the use of birth control pills. Women should take care not to exceed the recommended dosage of vitamin B_6, since nerve damage from overdose (2,000 mg or more daily) can occur. Many clinicians prescribe vitamin E to relieve breast pain, although there is no scientific proof that this vitamin actually does any good. But, as with lifestyle modifications, the cost and risk of vitamin and mineral supplements (in recommended amounts) is low enough to justify giving them a try.

Some symptoms of PMS may also be amenable to drug therapy. One of the problems plaguing the research on these treatments is the lack of a universally accepted definition of PMS and a universally accepted method of measuring symptoms. What this means is that studies are apt to involve a diverse group of women, many of whom may not actually have PMS or may have different forms of PMS—not all of which respond well to whatever medication is being tested. In addition, there is a considerable placebo effect in many of the drug studies—that is, the women taking "sugar pills" do just as well as the women taking the drug.

The few randomized clinical trials of medications published to date do afford some promise. Some of these trials involve drugs that treat specific symptoms of PMS. For example, taking nonsteroidal antiinflammatory drugs (such as ibuprofen or naproxen) can help relieve pelvic pain and may also reduce fatigue, mood swings, and headache. The diuretic drug spironolactone seems effective in relieving bloating and edema if taken during the luteal (second) phase of the menstrual cycle. Taking low doses of bromocriptine during this phase of the cycle seems to relieve severe breast pain.

Hormonal therapy can be effective, although the side effects may make it impractical. Drugs called GnRH (gonadotropin releasing hormone) analogs (such as Lupron or Synarel), for example, seem to relieve both physical and psychological symptoms of PMS. But, besides being very expensive, they cannot be used for more than 6 months without seriously compromising bone density; in the future it may be possible to overcome some of this effect by taking supplements of estrogen and progesterone. Bothersome side effects, including excess hair growth, acne, and hot flashes, also limit the use of danazol, a synthetic antiestrogenic hormone.

For years researchers in the field have had high hopes for progesterone supplements, but the results of the many studies so far are conflicting. Some studies indicate that taking progesterone may actually worsen premenstrual symptoms. As for birth control pills, these seem to affect only a small number of premenstrual symptoms. Yet, if a woman with PMS chooses to use the pill for contraception, she may be pleasantly surprised to find that some of her PMS symptoms disappear at the same time.

Finally, some psychotropic agents seem to relieve certain premenstrual symptoms. For example, using the antidepressant fluoxetine (Prozac) or one of its relatives appears to be beneficial, probably because it alters serotonin levels. Another drug that affects serotonin, fenfluramine, also seems to reduce depression and stem calorie, fat, and carbohydrate consumption in women with PMS. This drug, available in the United States as Redux, is more commonly prescribed for treatment of serious obesity.

The antianxiety drug alprazolam (Xanax) seems to alleviate both anxiety and depression, as well as physical symptoms, whether it is taken during the luteal phase or throughout the menstrual cycle. The chances of becoming dependent on this medication can be reduced by restricting its use to the luteal phase. There is also some limited evidence that the beta blocking drug atenolol may help relieve premenstrual irritability and may help reduce premenstrual migraine headaches.

Other treatment alternatives on the horizon may one day make it possible to avoid drug therapy. There has been some success, for example, in alleviating depression with bright light treatments or late sleep deprivation (awakening at 2 A.M.) as soon as symptoms begin.

If all else fails, and if symptoms are intolerable, hysterectomy (including the removal of both ovaries) is another option. This is a drastic solution that should not be undertaken without a second opinion from a physician experienced in the care of women with PMS.

Menopause

Menopause—popularly known as "the change of life," or simply "the change"—means the permanent cessation of the monthly menstrual period. The term is generally used to include a much larger set of events, however, both before and after the end of menstruation. All of these events—physical, emotional, and social—are related to a woman's changing hormone levels at midlife, which end the phase of life when childbearing is possible.

Once a taboo subject relegated to silent fears or, at best, private whispers between the closest of friends, menopause was for many years falsely associated with erratic mood swings, overwhelming depression, and the loss of sexual desire and pleasure. Only recently have these negative stereotypes begun to crumble, owing largely to the widespread attention now paid to menopause by popular books and magazines, television talk shows and specials, and government agencies such as the National Institutes of Health and the Office of Technology Assessment. As a result, menopause is increasingly being seen as a natural part of life, with both positive and negative aspects. Many women now readily discuss their observations and decisions about how to handle menopause with one another as well as with their clinicians.

One of the reasons why menopause has recently become a leading women's health issue has to do with changing demographics. Whereas a woman's average life expectancy at the turn of the twentieth century was only 50 years, today women can expect to live on average to about 78. Given that the typical woman undergoes menopause around age 51, this means that most women still have as much as a third of their life remaining after menopause begins. There are now some 40 million American women in or past menopause, and another 20 million women will reach it within the next decade as the baby boomers age.

Menopause is also being taken more seriously because of a better understanding of the serious impact it can have on a woman's health, as well as a renewed respect for quality of life issues. The problems of menopause were once dismissed as either vain or emotional, unworthy of serious medical attention. New evidence that physical changes after menopause significantly increase a woman's risk of developing debilitating, life-threatening, and costly diseases, particularly heart disease and bone fractures from osteoporosis, has put menopause in a whole new light.

▸ What are the "symptoms" of approaching menopause?

Although the average woman will go through menopause at the age of 51, the normal range of ages at which menopause may occur extends from 42 to 58. If a woman younger than 40 undergoes menopause naturally, she is said to be experiencing premature menopause. Women who undergo premature menopause should be carefully evaluated by a clinician to make sure that there is no disease underlying the changes. No known factor can predict whether an individual woman will undergo an early or a late menopause, with the exception of cigarette smoking: women who smoke experience menopause an average of 2 years earlier than nonsmokers. Whatever her age, a woman who has both her ovaries removed will undergo "surgical" menopause.

For 5 to 10 years before menstrual periods actually cease, the body begins to undergo various neuroendocrine and ovarian changes leading up to menopause. This period is called the perimenopausal transition. For reasons still little understood, it is marked by changes in the menstrual cycle: shorter periods, irregular periods, heavy menstrual flow, or a combination of all three, differing from month to month. Because many perimenopausal women are still ovulating (releasing an egg from the ovary) despite irregular periods, contraception is necessary until menses have stopped for at least one year.

During the perimenopausal period there is a gradual decline in the production of estrogen hormones by the ovaries. This decline accelerates as menopause approaches. As a result, changes occur in the many bodily tissues that are responsive to estrogen, including the vagina, vulva, uterus, bladder, urethra, breasts, bones, heart, blood vessels, brain, skin, hair, and mucous membranes. Even after menopause small amounts of estrogen continue to be produced by the adrenal glands, as well as by fatty tissue, which converts some of the androgens (virilizing hormones) produced by the adrenals into estrogen. There is some speculation that the release of estrogen by fatty tissue may help explain why heavier women seem to have relatively fewer menopausal symptoms.

Perhaps the most common of the symptoms associated with estrogen loss—affecting approximately 75 percent of women having a natural menopause and 90 percent of those having a surgical menopause—are hot flashes. Technically, a hot flash is the subjective feeling of warmth that a woman feels before there is any measurable change in her temperature. This is followed by the hot flush, a physiologically measurable change marked by visible redness and sometimes sweating in the chest, neck, and face.

Hot flushes are more common at night than in the daytime. These night sweats are often severe enough to interfere with sleep, and they seem to account for a good deal of insomnia among menopausal women. It is likely that many of the negative attributes once chalked up to menopause itself—mood swings, irritability, depression, fatigue—can be traced to the sleep disturbances caused by night sweats. Most people, male or female, who are awakened every time they are about to enter deep sleep will develop signs of emotional or mental instability. Hot flashes and flushes tend to subside with time and disappear after about 1 to 5 years, although in some women they last indefinitely.

Hot flushes are sometimes treated with estrogen replacement therapy. This therapy also protects women from coronary artery disease (the major killer of women) and osteoporosis (bone thinning). The pros and cons should be discussed with a primary care physician. Symptoms related to vaginal atrophy can be ameliorated with vaginal lubricants such as Replens, topical creams, Kegel exercises, and frequent intercourse. To minimize hot flushes, many women avoid factors that might precipitate problems—such as stress, hot weather, warm rooms, hot drinks, alcohol, caffeine, and spicy foods. Some studies have shown that paced deep breathing, acupuncture, biofeedback, and other relaxation techniques are helpful.

The reduction in estrogen levels often leads to vaginal atrophy—the drying and thinning of the tissues of the vagina and urethra. Many of the sexual problems once thought to be inevitable and irreversible aspects of menopause may simply be due to this phenomenon, which can produce vaginal inflammation, inadequate lubrication, and painful intercourse. When estrogen is not appropriate for a woman with hot flushes, her clinician may prescribe medroxyprogesterone acetate (Provera), a kind of progestin, or drugs that relax blood vessels, such as clonidine (Catapres) and beta blockers. Recent studies have shown promise with Megace (megestrol acetate), another progestational agent, in relieving the symptoms of menopause. Megace does not protect against osteoporosis or coronary artery disease, however.

Whatever decision is made about estrogen replacement therapy, menopause is an excellent time to reassess exercise, nutrition, and health care patterns with an eye to preventing chronic disease. For women who smoke, quitting cigarettes is the most powerful step they can take to reduce the risk of future heart disease, regardless of estrogen replacement use. For all women, having more frequent screenings of blood cholesterol, moderating alcohol intake, and eating a low-fat diet rich in fruits, vegetables, and whole grains makes good sense. To help prevent osteoporosis, the diet should also include 1,000 to 1,500 milligrams of calcium per day, as well as 400 to 800 international units of vitamin D. A regular program of weight-bearing exercise not only helps prevent osteoporosis but also contributes to maintaining an appropriate body weight. Vaginal atrophy is also associated with urinary symptoms that mimic urinary tract infections, including urinary frequency, painful urination, and stress incontinence (the involuntary loss of urine after laughing, sneezing, coughing, or vigorous exercise). At the same time, decreased estrogen levels predispose some women to true urinary tract infections (which can be prevented by estrogen replacement). A loss of muscle tone in the pelvic muscles—also related to declining estrogen levels—can exacerbate problems with incontinence and also increase the risk that the uterus, bladder, urethra, or rectum may protrude into the vagina.

Some women may notice increased growth of facial hair around menopause and a thinning of hair on the scalp. Sometimes women prone to adult acne find that it gets worse. These symptoms are attributed to the relative increase in the effects of testosterone, a virilizing hormone that is produced by the ovaries both before and after menopause.

There is no evidence that menopause itself predisposes women to depression. Women in their 20s and 30s are much more likely to develop a major depression than are older women. Nonetheless, the many life crises that can occur around the time of menopause may precipitate depression—including divorce, illness or death of parents, job loss, or children leaving home—as well as the very fact of aging in a society that values youth in women. At midlife a woman's focus may shift from the time lived to the time left to be lived. The prospect of mortality, sometimes underscored by the development of new medical problems, may contribute to mild melancholy in some women. Women who have a prolonged perimenopause with many symptoms also appear more prone to transitory depression.

Postpartum Emotions

The postpartum period is often defined as the first 6 weeks after childbirth. In reality, however, it takes many months or even longer (up to a year), depending on the individual woman, to work through all the emotional, physical, and social issues that occur after the birth of a baby.

Not all of these issues are problems, of course. The myth of the glowing new mother is not a complete fantasy: most mothers do experience intense and joyous feelings for their new babies, and many take pride in their ability to bear and nurture a child. Also, many women who have just had a baby feel a bond with other women for the first time in their lives or discover a new respect or love for their own mothers. For all the rewards of motherhood, however, having another person in the family almost always necessitates some changes in lifestyle, habits, and relationships. Though in the long run these changes are not necessarily for the worse, it is typical to experience some tension and turmoil until they are worked through.

The postpartum period can be a particularly vulnerable time for a woman's emotional and physical health. In the first weeks and months after birth, having sleep cycles interrupted, learning basic techniques of newborn care, and physically recovering from an arduous labor or a cesarean section (or both) virtually guarantee that no mother escapes fatigue. Breastfeeding, for all its virtues, makes additional demands on the mother's body and can contribute to fatigue, especially if she is not getting adequate nutrition and rest—which many new mothers are not. Even when the baby starts sleeping through the night and settles into a regular nap schedule (which may not happen for 6 months or more), taking care of the many needs of an infant or toddler continues to be physically draining. Women who already have one or more older children are likely to be even more exhausted: not only are opportunities to steal a nap few and far between, but also there are always more little people with needs that must be satisfied.

The classic piece of postpartum advice—repeated again and again

169

by doctors, nurse-midwives, health care manuals, and well-meaning relatives—counsels new mothers not to overlook their own needs. Nap when the baby naps, new mothers are told, let the housework go, accept all offers of help (casseroles, housecleaning, childcare), eat nutritiously without worrying about recovering your figure for a while, get some exercise, take relaxing baths, and tend to your personal health. Although women preach to one another about the importance of these things, they rarely follow their own advice.

Instead, affluent moms sign their children up for baby gym but claim they have no time to join a postpartum exercise class. They spend half an hour cutting up cantaloupe and tofu for their toddlers but subsist themselves on potato chips and diet soda. They buy stimulating toys and puzzles for their kids but spend their own free time scrubbing the toilet bowl. They meticulously bring their infants to the pediatrician every 2 months for checkups but skip having their teeth cleaned because it is too time-consuming. Other mothers—less financially secure—are self-sacrificing because they have little other choice: they have no safe and affordable childcare, no adequate parental leave from work, no family health insurance. For new mothers in this situation, the postpartum period is particularly stressful.

▸ Emotional adjustments

Adding a new person to a family and taking on the role as chief caregiver to that person can unleash a horde of unexpected and confusing feelings. In the first few days after delivery, inexplicable sadness and weepiness (the "baby blues") are as common as joy and exhilaration and are often attributed to the rapid readjustment of hormone levels. Some women develop postpartum psychiatric disorders (see above) in the weeks and months after giving birth. These involve much more serious symptoms of depression and psychosis. But for most women, the emotional issues of new motherhood revolve around self-doubts, loss of a sense of identity, boredom, stress on relationships with other family members (particularly one's partner), and ambivalence or frustration around the question of returning to work.

Early fears and self-doubt. Much more common in the early weeks after childbirth are feelings of inadequacy, fear, or panic that come when a first-time mother realizes that she is responsible for all aspects of a new human life or suspects that she does not have natural maternal feelings. In traditional societies new mothers were helped in their unfamiliar role by older and more experienced care-givers or by some form of communal childrearing arrangement. Today many women give birth hundreds or thousands of miles away from relatives, and few have the luxury of an accessible support system at their beck and call.

Today's mothers might take comfort in realizing that no human being is born knowing how to change a diaper, soothe the wails of colic, or give a bath to a slippery newborn. These skills can all be learned and developed with practice, however.

Loss of self. Women having their first baby may also find it difficult to incorporate their new role as mother with their previous roles. For the first time in her life, a woman may find herself completely ignoring her personal needs (sleep, food, conversation) for those of another person—and doing this day after day after day. It is common to spend an entire day busily tending to the baby's needs, all the while feeling that nothing whatsoever has been accomplished. Tasks that used to be routine—reading the newspaper, taking a shower, cooking a meal—suddenly become the main activity of the day, if they are achievable at all. As career plans, jobs, and hobbies are submerged by the needs of the baby, a woman may lose a sense of her individuality and fear that she is becoming that generic thing, a mother. Some of these feelings may eventually resolve, as the baby becomes more acclimated and the mother learns how to manage her time in new ways. In the meantime, sharing concerns with other new mothers can be beneficial.

Even the best, most organized mothers have occasional ambiva-lent or angry feelings toward their offspring because of the unceas-ing demands that come with motherhood. If a woman becomes seriously depressed or fears that she may harm herself or her infant, she needs to seek professional help as soon as possible.

Boredom. As the weeks go by, the mother who has tended the baby, cleaned the house from top to bottom, prepared the evening meal, and then finds herself with time to turn the mattresses may begin to notice that her initial fear and panic have been replaced by boredom. This is a problem especially for women who previously worked outside the home, but it can surface in any woman after the initial thrill of the new baby is gone. After the delivery truck stops arriving with gifts, and after friends stop popping in with casseroles, a new mother may begin to feel isolated from other adults. Accustomed to an outside job or regular social contact with peers, she may feel lonely spending all her time with a nonverbal little person whose needs are insatiable.

Many women find it helpful to join playgroups, where they can talk to other women in similar situations, or, at the very least express their feelings to close friends or relatives. If the budget allows, labor-saving tactics such as using disposable diapers or a diaper service, hiring an occasional babysitter, or paying for outside help with the housework can bring enormous relief. Sometimes it is possible to trade childcare with friends or share the cost of a babysitter with a few other families.

Jealousy, distancing, and other problems with partners. If a woman has chosen to stay home and care for the baby while her partner works outside the home, she may find that her interests and her partner's are drifting apart. She may feel hurt when the father shows little reaction to her tales of the baby's bowel problems or their visit to the pediatrician, while she may find that his accounts of office politics have become trivial and irrelevant. At the same time, the father may find himself becoming jealous of his partner's sudden devotion to, passion for, and physical closeness with the newborn, while the mother may be jealous of his achievements, contacts, and rewards in the outside world.

Communication is the first step in handling these feelings. It is crucial that new parents express their concerns to each other and try to work out new patterns of living. Perhaps the father can take an afternoon off once a week to watch the baby while the mother goes to exercise class or does some free-lance or volunteer work; or perhaps the household chores or cooking can be divided up differently. It is also a good idea for the parents to get out alone together as adults (even just to take a walk) at least once a week. Finding a mature babysitter whom she trusts and can call on for relief (without guilt) is one of the most important things a woman can do for herself and her relationship with her partner during the postpartum period.

Managing older children. Although a woman having a second or subsequent baby may not find caring for a newborn particularly daunting (although it is amazing how quickly these skills can be forgotten) and will have adjusted already to her role as mother, she still faces her own set of challenges. Just trying to balance the needs of the baby with the needs of the rest of the family can be tiring and unnerving. Many mothers feel disloyal toward their older children for putting the baby's needs first—or, conversely, feel guilty for thinking that they can never love this anonymous new person as much as their engaging older child.

Just how these feelings work themselves out varies considerably, not only with the personalities involved but also with the spacing and ages of the children. A mother with a toddler at home, for example, may be torn between her older child's skinned knee and the newborn at her breast—especially if the older child's needs had previously been fulfilled on demand. The mother may also have to spend considerable time guarding the baby against the jealous overtures of an older sibling as well as managing the related regressions of the older child—who may lose skills just gained in toilet training, sleeping through the night, temper control, and the like.

Even if siblings are older and not overtly jealous of (or are even helpful with) the newborn, it may be harder for a household geared toward the older children's carpool, homework, and school schedule suddenly to have to accommodate a baby's nap, feeding, and early rising demands—or deal with the consequences when this sort of accommodation is impossible. And frequently older children, while not openly jealous of the baby, will reflect their feelings by fighting more with one another. This can occur, for example, when the younger of two older siblings, previously quite close to the older one, not only loses her place as baby of the family but also loses the undiminished affection of her big brother or sister.

Some of these problems can be minimized by preparing the older children for the new baby. For toddlers, this may involve reading them stories about other children with new siblings, bringing them along to obstetrician visits, and showing them pictures of themselves as newborns. Preschoolers and school-age children might benefit from attending one of the many older sibling courses offered by hospitals. Asking older children to help with the newborn—fetching or changing a diaper, holding the baby, or whatever is appropriate—can work wonders in subduing feelings of jealousy and rejection. Finally, asking the father (or other relative) to play an expanded role in family life can ease some of the mother's burden.

Work and childcare. No blanket proclamations can be made about when (or if) a new mother should return to work. Physically, it is probably best for new mothers to stay home with the baby at least until the 6-week checkup—although some women bounce back to the daily routine within days of the delivery. Depending on a woman's individual circumstances, her clinician may recommend a more extended period of time away from work. Of course, many women have no choice in this matter for financial reasons or because they do not have access to day care. Among women who do have a choice, some prefer to stay home for a few months so that they have a chance to savor this fleeting period with their newborn or so that they can finish breastfeeding before returning to work (although women can certainly continue to breastfeed while working outside the home, especially if they use supplemental formula or pump and freeze their own milk). Still other women may be able to make part-time, flex-time, or job-sharing arrangements or may find ways to do part of their job at home.

Pregnant women should find out if they are eligible for maternity leave under the Family and Medical Leave Act (FMLA), which went into effect in August 1993. The act, which gave the United States the dubious distinction of being the last industrialized nation to provide family leave, gives workers of either sex the right to 12 weeks of unpaid leave in any calendar year to care for a new child or seriously ill family member, or to recover from personal illness. The employee is guaranteed her job and benefits back after the leave. One catch, however, is that employees are eligible for leave under this act only if their company has over 50 employees. The employee must also have worked for at least 1,250 hours in a single year at that company and can also be asked to cover the time away by giving up sick leave, personal days, and accumulated vacation days.

Needless to say, many people simply cannot afford to go 12 weeks without pay. Others fear that a request for leave may affect chances for promotion (or employment) somewhere down the line—which has been known to happen in spite of the law. This may be because, even though employers are theoretically required to provide eligibility criteria to their employees, very few employees or employers correctly understand their rights under this law, as shown in a recent study by 9 to 5 (the National Association of Working Women). To be fair, of course, many employers offer much more generous benefits than the bare minimum required by the FMLA, and it is worthwhile finding out just what they are well before the birth or adoption of a baby.

It is always a good idea to plan for childcare before the baby is born. Not only should a working woman investigate the childcare and maternity leave policies at her place of work (as well as actual experiences of co-workers), but also she should learn about other options for care, from live-in nannies and private babysitters to home day care and infant day care centers. Often arrangements for care must be made months in advance.

Even so, many women change their minds about work once the baby is born. An arrangement that looked good in the eighth month of pregnancy may take on a different aspect when the baby is suddenly a real person. The woman all set to return to work after 8 or 10 weeks' maternity leave may discover that she has fallen in love with her baby and cannot bear to tear herself away from the daily pleasures of mothering to go back to work. Other women, who vowed they would never leave their baby with a stranger, find themselves going crazy for lack of adult contact after only a month or two at home and may choose to look for a job or return to their former employment.

For all of these reasons, pregnant women and new mothers may want to keep their options about work and childcare open whenever possible. Instead of quitting her job, a pregnant woman might try to arrange for an extended maternity leave; several months down the road, after the baby is born, she can then reassess her needs and make a more informed decision than she could have made earlier about either returning to work or resigning. This is why it is also a good idea for working women to make childcare arrangements in advance of the birth, especially if high-quality infant care is scarce; a woman can always tell the day care provider later on that she has decided not to use the service. Finding good childcare at the last minute is stressful at best and often impossible. Even the loss of a deposit later on may be worth the peace of mind that comes from planning childcare in advance.

Insomnia

Insomnia, or the inability to get enough sleep, is an extremely common problem and can be a symptom of a host of physical and psychological disorders. Nevertheless, approximately a third of all people who think they have insomnia are actually getting enough sleep. Many people simply do not need the 8 hours of sleep that is often cited as ideal. Sleep needs among healthy people range from 4 to 10 hours, although the average adult gets between 7.5 and 8.5 hours of sleep per night. Also, as people age they sleep more lightly, with more frequent awakenings, and tend to need less sleep in general. This is partly so because certain medical problems—including certain kinds of heart disease and arthritis—can interfere with sleep, but also because sleep patterns change naturally over the course of one's life.

A good night's sleep consists of a series of sleep cycles, each representing a continuum of very light to very deep sleep and each lasting about 90 minutes. Throughout the night a sleeper goes back and forth from light to deep sleep a number of times. During the lightest phase, called non–rapid eye movement (or NREM) sleep, the sleeper is easily roused. It is in this stage that many people just beginning to doze may startle themselves awake, for example, after imagining a fall from some high place.

As a person passes through the NREM stages, sleep gradually deepens and at last reaches the deepest stage of the cycle, called rapid eye movement (or REM) sleep. In this stage the eyes begin to move vigorously under the lids, perhaps because they are "looking" at the dreams that occur at this time. Sleep researchers believe that to wake up feeling fully rested, a person needs an average of 4 uninterrupted sleep cycles consisting of both NREM and REM sleep. People with insomnia may go through too few sleep cycles per night to feel rested, or they may be missing out on some crucial part of each cycle—particularly REM sleep.

Although the purpose of sleep is still not fully understood, most researchers today believe that at least one of its roles is to give the body and brain time to recharge after the stress and strain of waking activity. Even so, the occasional episodes of sleeplessness that afflict virtually everyone at one point or another are rarely of deep concern. It is usually easy to make up for the lost sleep by dozing a bit longer once life has returned to normal, and most people who experience transient insomnia can expect to function relatively normally during the day and should not expect any long-term health consequences. The same is true for people who experience "sleep fragmentation," a phenomenon well known to most mothers (and more than a few fathers), who have had to get up for several brief periods during the night to care for an infant or a sick child.

Losing sleep for more than a few days, however, is another matter. People with either short-term insomnia (which can last for several weeks) or chronic insomnia (which can last for months or years) can experience a variety of problems, including excessive daytime sleepiness, lack of coordination, mental and physical sluggishness, poor judgment, impaired concentration, sensory deprivation, and dangerous behavior such as dozing behind the wheel of a car. A lack of deep, dream-filled (REM) sleep may also interfere with a person's ability to learn and to process the information garnered during the day. Dozing during the day can also keep a person from noticing and registering events going on around her. There is even some evidence that sleep-deprived people may have weakened immune systems that leave them more susceptible to colds and other illnesses.

▸ Who is likely to develop insomnia?

Among the many factors that can predispose a person to insomnia are emotional stress and anxiety, including the stress and anxiety that come from worrying about insomnia. Jet lag, conflicts at work, excitement or worry about a relationship or a new project—any of these can make sleeping difficult for a night or two. Traumatic life events such as the death of a loved one, the break-up of a relationship, the loss of a job, or the fear of having a serious illness can all induce short-term insomnia.

Chronic insomnia, by contrast, can result from underlying physical disorders (such as fibromyalgia) which make sleeping uncomfortable or from psychiatric problems, particularly depression. Although some depressed people sleep excessively, others find themselves waking in the wee hours of the morning. Shift workers who routinely alter sleeping and waking times, as well as people with sleep disorders such as "restless leg syndrome" or sleep apnea, may be prone to chronic insomnia as well.

Excessive caffeine consumption is classic cause of insomnia. Although most people realize that drinking a couple of cups of caffeinated coffee after dinner may interfere with sleep, they often forget that there is caffeine in tea, cola, and chocolate, not to mention a large number of over-the-counter drugs, including many allergy and arthritis medications, decongestants, cold remedies, and painkillers. Another medication that can keep women from sleeping is appetite suppressants. Finally, some people who take the older forms of beta blockers for high blood pressure, angina, and other heart problems are kept awake by the disturbing nightmares that are occasionally caused by these drugs.

Using over-the-counter sleep medications or alcohol to induce sleep may exacerbate insomnia. Alcohol induces sleep in the early part of the night, but it disrupts sleep later on. Over time, people develop a tolerance to both alcohol and over-the-counter sleep aids, so that increasingly large doses are needed to produce the same effect.

Bouts of sleeplessness are common during pregnancy. In the first trimester frequent trips to the bathroom in the middle of the night often interrupt sleep, and later in pregnancy vivid dreams, not to mention the difficulty of finding a comfortable position, can keep pregnant women from getting a good night's sleep. Once the baby is born, new mothers are chronically robbed of sleep, not necessarily because of insomnia per se but because they simply do not have time to get enough rest. Besides having to spend the wee hours of the night feeding a hungry newborn, a mother of young children is often busy running a household, chauffeuring kids to activities, managing the entire family's schedule, and possibly working a full-time or part-time job. A child who is sick or wakes with a bad dream—or a child who rises routinely at the crack of dawn—is often the source of a mother's sleep deprivation as well. Many new mothers sleep only 2 or 3 hours at a time and miss out on valuable REM sleep. A woman who suffers from postpartum depression is even more likely to have trouble sleeping.

Menopause is another time of life when insomnia becomes a problem for women. Here the source is usually hot flashes, which can be drenching and uncomfortable enough to rouse a woman from sleep several times during the night. Even in women unaware of nighttime hot flashes, a decrease in REM sleep related to falling estrogen levels can cause fatigue and occasionally can contribute to depression.

▸ What are the symptoms?
A person who is not getting enough sleep will generally doze—or think about dozing—whenever she is bored or inactive. She will often need an alarm clock to get out of bed in the morning and use caffeine to get through the day. Another common symptom of sleep deprivation is irritability with family, friends, and co-workers.

▸ How is the condition evaluated?
Anyone who feels excessively sleepy or fatigued during the day should suspect that she may have insomnia. Certain sleep disorders (particularly sleep apnea—which requires medical attention) can interfere with sleep while leaving the person unaware of the disruption.

If the cause of the insomnia is elusive, or if the insomnia may be due to a serious sleep disorder, a visit to a physician is prudent. A simple standardized test called the Multiple Sleep Latency Test (MSLT) can be performed to measure how long it takes for the person to fall asleep in a dark room. Normally it takes about 5 to 20 minutes to fall asleep under such conditions, but a sleep-deprived person may fall asleep in under 5 minutes. Of course, this test has its limitations, since a true insomniac may be sleep-deprived and still unable to fall asleep under test conditions.

A thorough evaluation of insomnia can be obtained at a sleep disorders center. These centers, which can be found at many major medical centers, offer a multidisciplinary approach to evaluating and treating sleep disorders. Specialists in fields such as neurology, psychiatry, and pulmonary medicine review the patient's symptoms and consider her medical and psychiatric history. Sometimes the source of the problem can be identified only if the patient undergoes one or more overnight tests in which brain waves, breathing, and eye and muscle movements are measured during sleep. These evaluations can be quite costly, although many health insurance policies will cover them.

▸How is insomnia treated?

Short-term insomnia can sometimes be helped with over-the-counter sleep aids (such as Sominex, Nytol with DPH, Nervine, Sleep-Eze, or Unisom) or even a glass of wine. Most over-the-counter sleep aids rely on the action of antihistamines, such as diphenhydramine (in Benadryl). It may be cheaper to buy generic antihistamines than sleep aid products, although it is essential to choose an antihistamine that does not contain agents to counteract drowsiness.

When nonprescription medications are no longer effective, a physician will usually prescribe benzodiazepine tranquilizers such as diazepam (Valium) or lorazepam (Ativan). Like all tranquilizers, these drugs can be addictive if used over long periods of time, and because they suppress the dream stage of sleep, withdrawal can result in "rebound" nightmares. Nevertheless, for insomnia associated with anxiety, a short course of tranquilizers can sometimes be helpful.

Some physicians may prescribe low doses of antidepressant drugs such as amitriptyline, trazodone, or doxepin instead. Although tolerance and rebound effects do not develop with these drugs, some people are bothered by side effects such as "drug mouth" or morning grogginess, even in low doses.

New drugs such as ambien can help with regularizing sleep cycles but can be used only for a couple of months. A natural hormone, melatonin, produced by the pineal gland, helps regulate sleep-wake cycles and other daily (circadian) body rhythms. Melatonin can now be obtained over the counter. It needs to be taken at precise times of the day because it alters the "set-point" for the sleep cycle. Melatonin can also be extremely helpful in preventing jet lag. (As an added benefit, it may have antioxidant effects and thus be an agent for cancer prevention.) A woman who suffers from chronic insomnia may want to ask her clinician about whether or not melatonin is appropriate.

Various nondrug strategies used under the supervision of a sleep specialist or other clinician may work better in the long run than sleeping pills. In chronotherapy, the hours of going to bed and waking up are gradually delayed until the biological clock is set to the desired time. Alternatively, various sleep restriction techniques can be used to extend gradually the time spent in bed. In these techniques the patient is first kept out of bed even when she is sleepy and forced to wake up before she is ready. Daytime naps are forbidden as well. Later she is allowed to wake up at her regular time but is forced to go to bed several hours later than usual until at last the time spent sleeping in bed has reached the desired level.

None of these techniques is effective if the insomnia is a symptom of some physical or psychological problem such as sleep apnea or depression. In such cases treatment for insomnia goes hand in hand with treating the underlying disorder. Estrogen replacement therapy is very effective in relieving the hot flashes that can cause insomnia during menopause.

▸ How can insomnia be prevented?

A great deal of insomnia can be prevented or alleviated without professional help. Good "sleep hygiene" is generally the first line of attack against insomnia. This consists of following certain low-cost, self-help techniques that often help promote drowsiness and regular sleep cycles.

Stick to a regular sleep-wake schedule. Do not try to make up for lost sleep on weekends or holidays. This seems to help because every person has a built-in biological clock which regulates sleepy and wakeful periods (as well as times of peak metabolism). If the clock is "set" for 11 P.M. sleepiness, and a person tries to go to sleep at 9 P.M., problems are bound to arise. The most notorious example is shift workers, who must go to sleep in daylight hours for part of the week and nighttime hours for another part.

Avoid sporadic naps. Although taking a nap at the same time every day can be helpful (by decreasing the need for sleep at night), frequent catnaps and dozing just end up disrupting nighttime sleep. The optimal time for napping is about 12 hours after the midpoint of usual nighttime sleep.

Wind down slowly before going to bed. Avoid stressful activities such as sorting unpaid bills or picking a fight with one's spouse. Some people find it relaxing to stroll about the house, write a letter, read a book, or take a warm bath before attempting to sleep. Relaxation exercises can also be helpful, but vigorous exercise after dinner should be avoided. One relaxation exercise that helps many people is lying in bed and progressively tensing and then relaxing each muscle group, starting with the toes and working up to the shoulders and neck. Other people find it helpful to do abdominal breathing, which involves keeping the chest still and using the stomach muscles to take slow deep breaths.

Make the bedroom conducive to sleep. A comfortable bed, attractive linens, dark windowshades, adequate ventilation, temperature and humidity control during all seasons, air filters for people suffering from allergies or asthma, and eye coverings or earplugs if necessary can all make sleep come more easily.

Leave the bedroom if sleep is a problem. The last thing a sleep-deprived person wants to do is build up an association between the bedroom and sleeplessness. If relaxation exercises do not work, instead of tossing and turning in bed one might try going to some other room to read quietly or watch a dull television program. The goal is to provide a relaxing, comforting, and quiet environment.

Exercise regularly. Exercise during the day seems to make sleep come easier at night. Daytime or at least early evening exercise is best, since vigorous activity right before bed can keep a person up for hours.

Be careful about food and drink. Eating meals at the same time every day can help synchronize the body's biological clock. Some people find that drinking warm milk or having a high-carbohydrate snack just before bed helps them sleep. Some researchers maintain that this is because such foods are high in L-tryptophan, a naturally occurring amino acid that seems to promote drowsiness. (High levels of L-tryptophan are also found in turkey, which may help explain the "turkey narcolepsy" that many people experience after Thanksgiving dinner.) There is no scientific evidence thus far that the amount of L-tryptophan in food is enough to alleviate anything more than the most minor insomnia, however. Higher doses, in supplement form, often produce nausea and other side effects and should be avoided.

Alcohol Addiction

The percentage of women addicted to alcohol has grown by leaps and bounds since the late 1960s. Today an estimated 4.6 million American women are alcoholics—that is, dependent on alcohol— and 1 out of every 3 alcoholics in this country is female. The increase in drinking among younger women is growing at a particularly high rate. As women make strides toward professional and educational equity, some of them seem to develop a pattern of "drinking like men," thus increasing their susceptibility to alcohol-related problems.

Yet the tenacious belief that respectable women are not heavy drinkers has made women less likely to admit they have a problem with alcohol; and many of them are less likely than men to drink heavily in public, where other people may discover it. Drinking clandestinely and alone, many women alcoholics are socially isolated, demoralized by the prolonged illness of alcoholism, and less likely than men to seek treatment for it.

Women who do admit they have a drinking problem may risk losing custody of their children. In recent years, some states have prosecuted women as criminals for exposing their children in utero to alcohol and other drugs. Women aware of these risks have even greater incentives to hide or deny their alcoholism.

Women who seek therapy get much less psychological and social support from spouses and other family members than do men. Women alcoholics not only are more likely than men to have an alcoholic spouse, but also are more likely to have other alcoholic family members for whom they are the caretakers. These women often develop depression, psychosomatic disorders, or eating disorders in addition to their drinking problem. Whereas only 1 in 10 married men who seek treatment for alcoholism ends up divorced, 9 out of 10 married women alcoholics are divorced after or during treatment.

Women are still less likely than men to be diagnosed by their physician as having a problem with alcohol, and therefore less likely to be treated for it. The notion that only certain types of women drink to excess has led physicians to overlook the drinking problems of many professional and well-educated women. Misdiagnosing alcoholism as depression or anxiety, they may end up prescribing mood altering and potentially addictive drugs that do not address the problem and can in fact make it worse. These drugs include other central nervous system depressants—such as barbiturates or tranquilizers—which, when mixed with alcohol, can lead to serious side effects.

▸ Who is likely to develop alcoholism?

In general, white women are more likely to use alcohol than are African American women, and both of these groups are more likely to drink than are Hispanic women. College graduates are more likely to drink than high school graduates.

People start drinking alcoholic beverages for many reasons, usually because drinking is part of social life in their circle. Some women may start drinking because they find that it helps them cope better with young children, job stress, separation, divorce, or bereavement. Others may begin using alcohol to relieve aches and pains or insomnia. Teenage girls with low self-esteem or impaired ability to cope with stress may drink to relieve shyness, to increase their enjoyment of dates, or simply to "get high." For reasons still not fully understood—but which probably have to do with biological differences—only some of these people will end up as alcohol abusers or alcohol-dependent.

Single, divorced, or separated women are more likely to drink heavily and have alcohol-related problems than are married women or widows (although cause and effect are not easy to disentangle). Alcohol abuse and dependence in women is often associated with depression, and more often than not the depression preceded the alcohol problems. Perhaps related to the depression is the fact that women with alcoholism attempt suicide more often than other women. Alcohol abuse seems to be particularly common among young women, although older women with a drinking problem may simply be harder to identify. Women with histories of childhood sexual abuse are more likely than others to become alcoholics later in life.

Other risk factors for alcoholism include having a personality disorder, having biological relatives who are alcoholics, and working in an environment that encourages heavy drinking.

▸ What are the symptoms?

Alcohol abuse and dependence means the repetitive and chronic use of alcohol to the point where it significantly interferes with an individual's health or the ability to function normally. People who are dependent develop a tolerance to alcohol and require increasing amounts of it to achieve the same effects. They also suffer from withdrawal symptoms when they reduce or stop their alcohol intake. These can include the classic hangover—headache, nausea, vomiting, anxiety, or malaise. In cases of heavy drinking, the end result may be DTs (delirium tremens)—tremors, panic attacks, confusion, delirium, hallucinations, and seizures.

In addition to increased tolerance and symptoms of withdrawal, other signs of alcohol dependence include a preoccupation with drinking, excessive or frequent drinking, solitary drinking, and temporary memory lapses (blackouts). Using alcohol as a medicine or to promote sleep, making excuses for drinking, or denying that drinking is a problem despite evidence to the contrary are other signs (see chart).

Some background may be helpful. Alcohol (ethyl alcohol or ethanol) is a naturally occurring colorless liquid produced by the fermentation of sugars. A central nervous system depressant, it acts as a sedative or tranquilizer that relaxes people and releases their inhibitions. Although people who have had a drink or two may feel more confident and talkative, the alcohol is actually slowing down their motor coordination and reaction time, as well as impairing judgment, memory, reasoning, and self-control. These effects are more obvious when large quantities of alcohol are consumed. Too much alcohol can lead to drowsiness, stupor, and life-threatening coma.

Studies find that women have higher blood alcohol levels than men after drinking the same amount, even after adjusting for body weight. Because women generally have a higher ratio than men of body fat to water, there is proportionately less water available in the female body in which alcohol can be dispersed. Women also have relatively low levels of an enzyme called gastric alcohol dehydrogenase, which is responsible for breaking down alcohol in the stom-

> ## How to recognize a possible drinking problem
>
> Have you ever tried to cut down on your drinking?
> Has criticism of your drinking ever annoyed you?
> Have you ever felt guilty about your drinking?
> Have you ever had an "eye opener"?

ach. Alcohol seems to be more rapidly absorbed into the blood-stream at certain points of the menstrual cycle, particularly just before the menstrual period.

Because of alcohol's effects on the nervous system, women under the influence of alcohol may engage in risky behaviors or make mistakes they would normally avoid. For example, they may forget to use birth control or neglect to insist on condom use by a new sexual partner. Women who drink heavily are more likely to become victims of alcohol-related violence, including domestic abuse and rape. In addition, 30 to 70 percent of women alcoholics are dependent on other drugs, including sedatives and minor tranquilizers.

Alcohol-related health problems appear much sooner and more severely in women than in men. Women develop cirrhosis of the liver (a progressive disease that causes permanent liver damage) over a shorter period of time and they die from it at a younger age than do men—despite the fact that they tend to drink less overall and tend to develop a drinking problem at a later age than men do. Both Native American and African American women have particularly high rates of cirrhosis.

In addition to cirrhosis, the Harvard Nurses' Study confirmed the association between heavy drinking and a woman's risk of dying from cancer, particularly breast cancer. Cancers of the mouth, throat, larynx, esophagus, stomach, and pancreas are also more common among heavy drinkers. Other health problems that have been linked to alcoholism are fatty liver, obesity, anemia, malnutrition, and peptic ulcers.

Alcohol consumption can worsen osteoporosis, a disorder leading to progressive loss of bone density and accompanying fractures. One study found that women over 65 who drank 2 to 6 drinks per week had an increased risk of hip fracture, both because they were more likely to fall and because of the effects of alcohol on bone strength.

Women who are heavy drinkers seem to have high rates of amenorrhea, abnormal vaginal bleeding, painful menstrual cramps, premenstrual syndrome, infertility, and—although drinkers may feel more aroused after a glass of wine—sexual dysfunction (including vaginal pain, lack of sex drive, and inability to have an orgasm). Whether these problems are due to drinking alcohol or are a reason for drinking in the first place remains unclear.

Recently the effects of alcohol on a growing fetus have received a lot of publicity. The most severe complication that can occur from drinking more than 4 drinks per day during pregnancy is called fetal alcohol syndrome (FAS). In this condition the affected infant develops irreversible mental retardation, which leads to later learning disabilities, coordination and balance problems, and hyperactivity. Babies born with this syndrome have an unusually small head (microcephaly) and a depressed nose bridge, an elongated and flattened upper lip, abnormally small eyes, and displaced, deformed ears. Defects of the joints, limb, or organs, including congenital heart defects or malformed hips, often occur in FAS.

Moderate drinking (under 2 drinks per day) in pregnant women has been linked to prematurity, low birth weight, and more subtle neurological problems. Even occasional social drinking may increase the risk of miscarriage, particularly during the first trimester of pregnancy. Experiments in animals suggest that binge drinking is more dangerous than consuming small amounts of alcohol over a long period of time.

In light of these serious risks, obstetricians recommend total abstinence during pregnancy, since no one knows the level of alcohol that can be consumed safely (and this may vary from woman to woman).

▸ How is alcoholism treated?

Only about a fourth to a fifth of all patients in treatment for drinking problems are female, even though about a third of all alcoholics are women. Many women with alcoholism are clearly not getting the treatment they need.

Once a woman has been diagnosed as having a problem with alcohol—and, most crucially, has admitted to herself that she is alcohol-dependent—treatment can begin. Women who have support at home and are not at risk of losing child custody or a job may first ask their clinician to refer them to a 12-step program such as Alcoholics Anonymous, Al-Anon (for the spouses of alcoholics), Women for Sobriety, Rational Recovery, and Secular Organizations for Sobriety. All-women, all-lesbian, or all-nonsmoker self-help groups of the 12-step variety are available.

Whether or not a woman chooses to enter a 12-step program, her clinician should also work with her to achieve detoxification (a process through which the woman is weaned from alcohol), provide any necessary medical care to aid the withdrawal process, and help her find better ways to deal with stress, anxiety, anger, and other emotions. Often family therapy is useful in educating other family members about the disease and helping them handle their negative feelings about the patient and participate in the recovery process. Psychiatric illnesses such as major depression which often accompany alcoholism need to be treated separately, usually with a combination of psychotherapy and antidepressants.

If a woman has more severe medical problems, an abusive home situation, legal issues, or a partner or other immediate family member who is a substance abuser, the clinician may refer her to an alcohol treatment clinic, detoxification center, hospital, or residential care facility, where appropriate specialists are available. Often the staff will include recovering alcoholics who serve as role models in addition to providing professional care. These facilities can provide treatment on an outpatient or inpatient basis as appropriate.

Part of the recovery program at alcohol treatment clinics involves education about balanced diet and the nature of alcoholism, and group therapy or self-help groups. Individual counseling or other psychotherapy may be provided as well. Medical supervision is necessary if drugs such as benzodiazepines (Librium, Valium) are given to help prevent DTs.

Sometimes a drug called disulfiram (Antabuse), which disrupts the metabolism of alcohol in the liver, may be useful in preventing alcohol consumption. After a person takes tablets of this drug, con-suming alcohol (even the small amount contained in some foods, mouthwashes, and cough syrups) results in extremely unpleasant physical reactions, including flushing, nausea, severe vomiting, throbbing headaches, sweating, chest pain, rapid heartbeat, diffi-culty breathing, blurred vision, and dizziness. The purpose of the drug is to serve as a powerful physical deterrent to alcohol consump-tion, but it works over the long run only if the patient takes it willingly.

Almost all treatment programs view alcoholism as a chronic, pro-gressive disease and insist on complete abstinence from alcohol and other addictive substances. Some aftercare programs are available to help recovering alcoholics remain sober and to help them if relapse occurs. Many experts recommend using a self-help group such as Alcoholics Anonymous as a support system.

Not everyone views alcoholism as treatable only with abstinence, however. A return to "social" (or "controlled" or "asymptomatic") drinking is the goal of some programs, and a handful of studies have demonstrated that a tiny minority of alcohol abusers can learn to control their drinking behavior for long periods of time. A large-scale study that sheds light on the question of abstinence versus controlled drinking—the ongoing Harvard Study in Adult Develop-ment, which has been following a large sample of (male) Harvard graduates for many decades—has found that the success rate of those who have attempted to drink asymptomatically has been far from impressive over the long term. The Harvard investigators have concluded that, while it is possible for a few alcohol-dependent people to return to social drinking for a period of time, controlled drinking is, in most cases, a transient stage between abstinence and abuse. A more practical treatment goal for the vast majority of problem drinkers is to avoid alcohol entirely.

▸ Alcohol and heart disease

In the last decade or so considerable controversy has arisen about whether women who drink moderate amounts of alcohol might actually be healthier than either nondrinkers or heavy drinkers. Until recently the evidence in favor of alcohol came largely from studies on men, and it indicated that drinking 2 alcoholic beverages a day significantly reduces deaths from clogged heart arteries—probably because alcohol increases levels of high-density (HDL) cholesterol and reduces the formation of plaque in blood vessels. (These findings, in turn, fed speculations about the "French paradox": perhaps it was the red wine along with meals that explained why the French, with their cream-laden cuisine, were not unusually prone to heart disease.)

Most clinicians hesitated to extend these findings to women, however, partly because women are known to metabolize alcohol somewhat differently than men (accumulating more alcohol in their blood more readily) and partly because women who drink may be particularly susceptible to alcoholic liver disease and breast cancer.

It now appears that light to moderate drinking may indeed decrease deaths from all causes in women over the age of 50. A major 12-year study of 86,000 nurses aged 34 to 59 (part of the ongoing Harvard Nurses' Health Study) showed that women over 50 who drank between 1 and 20 drinks per week had a lower risk of death, particularly from cardiovascular disease, than nondrinkers. Heavier drinking (more than 20 drinks per week) was associated with an increased risk of death from other causes, particularly cirrhosis and breast cancer. (One drink = 12 ounces of beer = 5 ounces of wine = 1.5 ounces of 80-proof liquor. All of these are equivalent to 0.5 ounces or 12 grams of ethanol.)

The benefits were greatest for women who were at risk for heart disease—for example, women who were obese, smoked cigarettes, or had high cholesterol levels, high blood pressure, diabetes, or a family history of heart disease. Women 34 to 39 years of age who drank had a slightly higher risk of death from all causes regardless of how much they drank, but the number of deaths in this group was small.

This large and convincing study did not suggest that a nondrinker who suddenly adds a few drinks to her diet will necessarily lower her risk of cardiovascular disease. The benefits appeared only in women over 50 who were already drinkers when the study began. As in all studies of this type, it is possible that the lower death rates were attributable not to alcohol per se but to some other (unknown) factor common among women who drink moderately over the course of their adult lives. The only way to know for sure that alcohol itself confers health benefits would be to conduct a prospective study in which a group of nondrinkers started to drink moderately and were compared over time to an otherwise similar group who continued to abstain. Such a study seems unlikely.

If one adds to this research limitation the fact that women under 50 and risk-free women in the study showed no benefit from moderate drinking, and the fact that heavy drinking substantially increases a woman's risk of death, it does not make sense for nondrinkers to start drinking alcohol for the sake of their health. But for those women who already drink in moderation, most experts believe that they can continue in good conscience without worrying about serious health complications.

Substance Abuse

Substance abuse involves the use of drugs or other chemicals to the point where physical, psychological, or social functioning is impaired. Although the term is often associated with the use of illegal drugs such as marijuana and cocaine, it can also mean excessive reliance on legal substances such as alcohol or nicotine, prescription medications, and even certain over-the-counter products. Prescription medications such as minor tranquilizers, painkillers, and diet pills are much more commonly abused by women than is either alcohol or street drugs.

▸ Types of substance abuse

The federal government classifies all drugs with the potential for abuse under the Controlled Substances Act. There are 5 separate categories (schedules) of drugs, grouped by likelihood that the drug will cause dependence and other harmful effects.

Schedule I includes drugs (such as heroin) with the highest risk and which have no accepted medical use (even for research) or accepted level of safe use.

Schedule II drugs also have a high potential for abuse but are sometimes acceptable for use in medical research. These drugs include codeine and morphine (derived from opium), cocaine, marijuana, and phencyclidine (PCP, or angel dust).

Schedule III drugs are legally available by prescription to treat specific medical problems. Examples include diet pills, certain hypnotic-sedative drugs, and medications that combine narcotics with other drugs (Percocet and Percodan, for example).

Schedule IV includes barbiturate sleeping pills such as pentobarbital (Nembutal) and minor tranquilizers, including the benzodiazepines (Xanax, Valium, Klonopin).

Schedule V, the group of drugs with the lowest potential for abuse, includes certain drugs containing small amounts of codeine used to treat coughs or pain (such as Tylenol with codeine) or containing small amounts of paregoric to treat diarrhea (such as Parepectolin).

▸ Abuse of illegal drugs

A national household survey by the National Institute on Drug Abuse showed that about 5 percent of all women—in contrast to 8 percent of all men—report regularly using illegal drugs. The highest prevalence of use was reported in women of childbearing age, 8 percent of whom use illegal drugs, marijuana being the most common. An estimated 3 to 17 percent of pregnant women use cocaine.

Higher than average levels of use are reported among women who live in the inner city or who have criminal records, as well as among lesbians and women in the military. It should be pointed out, however, that these are women who (unlike middle-class homemakers) are at greatest risk of being "caught" abusing drugs. In some inner cities more women than men use crack, a highly purified and fast-acting form of cocaine. Women with college degrees are more likely to use cocaine than are those with only high school degrees.

The risk of acquiring a sexually transmitted disease, including acquired immune deficiency syndrome (AIDS), is increased in women who abuse illegal substances. Intravenous drug abuse has been involved in 80 percent of the AIDS cases that have occurred in women. Although occasionally women acquire AIDS through direct infection by a contaminated needle, most of the cases occur because women under the influence of drugs or alcohol tend to engage in risky sexual behaviors—including sex with a male IV drug user infected with the AIDS virus. Some investigators have linked the recent rise in the incidence of syphilis to the use of cocaine and other drugs.

Abuse of opiates, cocaine, and some other illegal substances can produce various forms of sexual dysfunction. Despite the common perception that certain drugs such as cocaine, heroin, or amphetamines (uppers or pep pills) can enhance sexual functioning, chronic use of these drugs can inhibit orgasms and decrease sexual desire (libido). Dependence on heroin can also suppress ovulation (the monthly release of an egg from an ovary). Although menstrual periods often return to normal after a few months of maintenance treatment with methadone (a substitute narcotic used to treat heroin addiction), methadone itself depresses sexual interest and response. Some tests indicate that marijuana use may also cause irregular menstrual cycles and a temporary loss of fertility.

Using cocaine while pregnant increases the risk of certain complications of pregnancy, including placenta previa (a condition in which the placenta covers the cervix and is prone to bleeding), placenta abruptio (a condition in which the placenta abruptly separates from the endometrium), intrauterine growth retardation, premature labor, and stillbirth. There is evidence linking cocaine use during pregnancy to numerous birth defects, including neural tube defects and malformations of the genitourinary, gastrointestinal, and cardiovascular systems of the fetus. The effect of cocaine on the neuropsychological development of children is less clear because studies so far have not ruled out nutritional, social, or other factors that might explain these developments.

One dangerous myth about cocaine use during late pregnancy has led some young women to use this drug in the hope that it will shorten their labor and make it less painful. This false belief stems from cocaine's stimulant and vasoconstrictive properties. Rather than facilitating labor, these properties have been linked to sudden death in pregnant women and to premature rupture of membranes, premature labor, and fetal distress (see chart).

‣ Abuse of prescription drugs

The major substance abuse problem for women is prescription mood altering drugs, particularly sedatives and minor tranquilizers. Mood altering drugs are prescribed at an earlier age in women than in men, and prescribed more frequently. This is partly because women are more likely to suffer from depression and anxiety than are men, because they may be more likely to seek help for psychological and emotional problems, and because some physicians resort to medications for personal problems that might be better treated with psychotherapy or other forms of social support. Among women alcoholics, 30 to 70 percent are also dependent on other drugs, including sedatives and minor tranquilizers.

Women are also at risk for dependency on analgesics (painkillers). Analgesics fall into two categories—narcotic and nonnarcotic. The nonnarcotics are not addictive and include drugs such as aspirin and

Known effects of substance abuse during pregnancy

Type of drug	Growth retardation	Behavior changes	Birth defects	Increased fetal or newborn death	Withdrawal in newborn	Premature birth
Opiates	Yes	Yes	No	Yes	Yes	No
Alcohol	Yes	Yes	Yes	Yes	Yes	Yes
Nicotine	Yes	Yes	No	Yes	No	Yes
Cocaine	Yes	Yes	Yes	Yes	Yes	Yes
Barbiturates	No	Yes	No	No	Yes	No
Stimulants	No	Yes	No	No	No	Yes
Hallucinogens	No	Yes	No	No	No	No
Marijuana	No	Yes	No	No	No	No
Minor tranquilizers	No	No	No	No	Yes	No
Major tranquilizers	No	No	Yes	No	No	No

acetaminophen (Tylenol). The narcotic drugs, which include opium derivatives such as codeine and morphine, are addictive and therefore have a much higher risk of abuse, especially among those who suffer from chronic pain syndrome—a problem more common in women than in men (see Psychosomatic Disorders).

The pervasive concern with weight among women in our culture sometimes leads them to take diet pills (amphetamines) without regard for their huge potential for addiction—and extremely limited potential for long-term weight loss. Women also commonly take these drugs for chronic fatigue and other sleep disorders. Although low doses can suppress the appetite and increase alertness, tolerance to the drug develops within weeks. As larger doses are taken to produce the same effects, women may become irritable, anxious, or overconfident, and various physical symptoms may occur, including blurred vision, dizziness, and insomnia. Chronic use of amphetamines can permanently damage the heart and blood vessels and result in a number of health problems, including various psychiatric symptoms, malnutrition, and an increased susceptibility to infection.

Prescription drug abuse is a particular problem for elderly women because aging makes people more sensitive to drugs. Doses that pose no problem in younger women become "overmedication" in older ones and lead to significant side effects. Even more pervasive in older women is the problem of multiple drug use, which occurs when people take several medicines at once. Tranquilizers and sedatives, frequently used by older people, can be especially dangerous if mixed with other drugs that depress the central nervous system. (A high rate of hip fractures in older women, for example, has been linked with overuse of minor tranquilizers, which can cause falls.) The problem of multiple drug use is compounded by the fact that many older women who see more than one physician hesitate to ask questions about possible drug interactions for fear of seeming to question the doctor's authority.

Virtually any drug taken during pregnancy (or breastfeeding) has the potential for some effect on the growing fetus (or infant). This does not mean that pregnant or nursing women should not take the medications they need to care for their own health; often the benefits will be found to outweigh the risks. But it does mean that any woman who is pregnant should consult her clinician before taking any drug—even seemingly harmless over-the-counter medications.

▸ Who is likely to abuse drugs and other substances?

Women with family members who abuse substances, women who started using drugs or alcohol early in life, and those who have been prescribed a mood altering drug (such as a tranquilizer, antidepressant, or sedative) are at risk for developing a substance abuse problem. Other risk factors include nicotine dependence, eating disorders, and a history of rape, incest, or physical molestation during childhood. Younger women who abuse drugs are also more likely than other women to be victims of domestic abuse and rape.

Women who abuse substances have a high rate of psychiatric illness such as depression and of attempted suicide, although no one knows if these are causes or effects of the substance abuse. Female substance abusers are also more likely than other women to have family and marital problems, whereas for men substance abuse more commonly leads to high rates of legal and job-related problems. Women substance abusers frequently end up divorced after seeking treatment.

▸ What are the symptoms?

People who are dependent on drugs develop a tolerance to them, that is, they require larger and larger doses to create the same effect. They also become addicted, which means that they experience physical or psychological symptoms of withdrawal when they stop or reduce their intake of the substance.

Besides the symptoms of tolerance and withdrawal, other behavioral indications that a person may have a problem with substance abuse include being unable to reduce usage, feeling guilty about the habit, or denying that there is a problem even when the effects on work or interpersonal relationships are obvious. Defensiveness when a friend expresses concern about drug use, using the drug to deal with interpersonal or work problems, changing doctors in order to get a prescription for the drug, mixing drugs and alcohol, or needing the drug to get going in the morning or to get to sleep each night are other signs of dependence.

Symptoms of drug abuse and withdrawal

Type of drug	Common symptoms of overuse or abuse	Common symptoms of withdrawal
Antidepressants (tricyclic antidepressants such as Tofranil, Elavil, Sinequan, and Aventyl)	Dry mouth Constipation Urinary retention Blurred vision Weight gain Drowsiness	Nausea Headache
Minor tranquilizers (such as Valium, Librium, Xanax)	Drowsiness Incoordination Confusion Rashes Constipation Menstrual changes Reduced sex drive	Nausea Headache Jitteriness Insomnia
Amphetamines (pep pills, diet pills, stimulants)	Overconfidence Excitability Irritability Anxiety Sweating Insomnia Blurred vision Dizziness Diarrhea	Suicidal depression Lethargy Fatigue Anxiety Nightmares
Barbiturates (sleeping pills, including Amytal, Butisol, Nembutal, Seconal)	Grogginess Headache Impaired motor function	Seizures Anxiety Weakness Insomnia Sweating

(continued)

Type of drug	Common symptoms of overuse or abuse	Common symptoms of withdrawal
Alcohol	Lack of coordination Stupor Coma Impaired judgment Memory loss Blackouts Release of inhibitions	Headache Nausea, vomiting Anxiety Malaise Tremors Panic attacks Confusion Delirium tremens Hallucinations Seizures
Marijuana, hashish	Increased pulse Relaxation Mild euphoria Diarrhea Chest pains Panic attacks Slowed reaction time Apathy Impaired judgment Disorientation Delirium Hunger Dry mouth, throat Feeling of unreality Confusion Paranoia	Tremors Sweating Nausea, vomiting Diarrhea Irritability Sleep disturbances Decreased appetite Tremor Chills

(continued)

Type of drug	Common symptoms of overuse or abuse	Common symptoms of withdrawal
Cocaine, crack	Sense of euphoria Increased alertness Dilated pupils Rapid heart rate Rapid breathing Temperature increase Paranoid hallucinations Confusion Slurred speech Anxiety Agitation Chest pain Seizures	Depression Confusion Irritability Seizures
Hallucinogens (such as LSD, mescaline)	Altered perceptions Increased heart rate Hypertension Impaired memory Shortened attention span Impaired thinking Excitability Incoordination Analgesia Insomnia Lack of appetite	None

(continued)

Type of drug	Common symptoms of overuse or abuse	Common symptoms of withdrawal
Phencyclidine (PCP)	Hallucinations Euphoria or mood swings Lack of coordination Slurred speech Jerky eye movements Feeling of weightlessness Sweating Muscle rigidity Disorganized thinking Drowsiness Stupor Coma Apathy Violent behavior Paranoia Breathing difficulties Convulsions	Lethargy Craving Depression
Narcotics (addictive analgesics or painkillers such as opiates— morphine, methadone, heroin)	Confusion Drowsiness Sedation Dizziness General weakness Sweating Lack of coordination Euphoria Decreased sex drive Coma Seizures Slowed breathing	Diarrhea Tremor Nervousness Drop in blood pressure Muscle pain Insomnia Nightmares Nausea Yawning Dilated pupils

(continued)

Type of drug	Common symptoms of overuse or abuse	Common symptoms of withdrawal
Inhalants (such as amyl nitrite, room deodorizers, Freon, benzene, nitrous oxide, glue	Headaches Dizziness Increased heart rate Nasal irritation Cough Muscle weakness Vomiting Abdominal pain Confusion Paralysis of nerves Itching	None reported
Laxatives	Chronic constipation	Constipation

Common physical symptoms of substance abuse—which vary according to the substance (see chart)—include anxiety, heart palpitations, depression, insomnia, fatigue, sexual dysfunction, abdominal pain, unexplained weight loss, bloodshot eyes, sweating, skin flushing, and, in women, a variety of menstrual complaints. Substance abuse can also underlie mood swings, loss of appetite, apathy, or a distant demeanor. Some people who abuse substances have no obvious symptoms.

▸ How is the condition treated?
Treating substance abuse is usually a long-term process that involves changing deeply rooted habits and confronting complex emotional or social problems. Because abuse is a disease that occurs in people with a biological predisposition, the afflicted person usually must learn how to avoid the abused substance for the rest of her life. Programs offered by rehabilitation centers, residential treatment facilities, and outpatient clinics can help facilitate the process of detoxification—the systematic and gradual withdrawal of the drug—and also provide support and education about drug use. The ideal

program is tailored to a woman's individual circumstances and includes psychotherapy to address any issues of self-esteem, sexual abuse, and interpersonal relationships that may underlie the substance abuse problem. Many women also find that self-help fellowships such as Cocaine Anonymous, Narcotics Anonymous, or Nar-Anon (for families of substance abusers) are helpful in providing long-term support and preventing relapses.

All of these resources are greatly underused by women, especially pregnant women. Part of the problem stems from the failure of many clinicians to recognize substance abuse in women; symptoms are attributed instead to depression or anxiety. Also playing a role is a lack of childcare in many treatment facilities. A few programs are starting to admit both mothers and children, but they are still few and far between. Cost and lack of adequate insurance coverage can also make many facilities inaccessible to women, particularly those who are single, unemployed, or employed in low-wage jobs.

Another problem that keeps women from seeking help is the fear of losing custody of their children, especially if they have to involve a public agency in their care. Infants have been removed from mothers who had a single positive drug test, even before any effort was made to diagnose or treat the problem. Owing to misplaced concern about the effects of illegal drugs on a fetus, women have been arrested and jailed for "delivering controlled substances to a minor." Instead of preventing substance abuse (which cannot be accomplished simply through an act of will), these efforts have kept other women—many of whom are already suspicious of the medical care system—from seeking the prenatal and postnatal care that could help both themselves and their children. Efforts are now being made in a few states to promote treatment of chemical dependency in lieu of this counterproductive prosecution.

Body Image

Body image is a person's inner perception of her own physical being. This image may or may not correspond to objective reality. It is perfectly possible—and quite common—for women within normal weight ranges to perceive themselves as grossly obese; this is a particularly severe problem in women who have anorexia nervosa and bulimia nervosa. It is also quite possible for women who have unexceptional features to believe that their noses are too big or their lips too thin. Study after study indicates that American women tend to be dissatisfied with their looks, rating themselves too ugly, too plain, too old, too pimply, too fat, too hairy, too tall, and so on. By contrast, men in general tend to be much more satisfied with their bodies, even when objective measurements indicate they might not meet certain standards of perfection.

It is often said that women are much more sensitive than men to certain aspects of their physical selves, perhaps because their daily lives are touched by bodily functions such as menstrual cycles, pregnancy, and childbirth, not to mention the natural functions of children and other people in their care. Whatever the explanation, it is undeniable that in women a poor body image can become an obsession so strong that it takes precedence over all other aspects of life. A poor body image is not merely a problem of women who are concerned about their sexual attractiveness but seems to be closely tied to women's overall sense of self-esteem and well-being.

A chronic dissatisfaction with physical appearance can be related to all sorts of health problems in women. Women with a negative body image are prone to develop anorexia, bulimia, or obesity, for example. In addition, many women who are unhappy with their physical selves often experience sexual dysfunction, since sexual arousal depends to a large extent on feeling attractive and desirable. And finally, a number of the products and services women purchase to improve or alter their appearance—from shoes to cosmetics to liposuction—can lead to physical problems in their own right.

▸ Body image and culture

Women throughout history and in many cultures have subjected themselves to a myriad of mutilations in the name of physical attractiveness—including foot binding and skin stretching. In modern America, women's chronic dissatisfaction with their bodies has fed a vast industry consisting of products and services that ostensibly improve a woman's appearance—and, implicitly or explicitly, her sex appeal. The consumer culture survives in part by creating solutions to physical problems that women may otherwise never be aware they have. The problem of vaginal "freshness" (or lack thereof), for example, was created by the manufacturers of feminine hygiene sprays.

Many of these products and services come at a cost to the body as well as the wallet. Feminists as far back as the nineteenth century have pointed out the damage women do to their bodies by binding their waists or breasts in tight foundation garments or cramming their feet into stylish footwear. Diet pills can lead to addiction, and some liquid diet products have led to serious heart problems and death. Many cosmetics and fragrances can irritate skin or provoke allergic reactions. Plastic surgery to alter facial features, to lift, reduce, or enlarge breasts, or even to suck the fat out of stomachs and thighs carries health risk as well as cosmetic benefits.

Not all of the problems women have with body image can be blamed on commercial advertisers, however. Some of women's compulsive behavior regarding appearance can be justified as a reasonable reaction to realities built into the world around them. Study after study seems to confirm that—like it or not—looks play a larger part in a heterosexual female's sexual attractiveness than in a heterosexual male's. For men, power and wealth seem more crucial attributes when it comes to wooing the other sex. Whether this difference is biological or cultural (or even attributable in part to the consumer culture) is a topic of hot debate, but whatever the explanation, for the time being it seems to be a fact of life.

A woman's attractiveness can have an effect on her grades in school and her employability after she is out in the working world. Sometimes these effects are unspoken or even unconscious. It just happens that the better-looking people (according to our society's standards of beauty) seem to get the better grades or get hired for the job. Sometimes the effects are overt—as when an employer requires that all female workers wear makeup or skirts or meet a specific weight requirement. Some of these requirements are being overturned in courts of law.

In short, women are judged by higher standards than are men when it comes to looks. This makes it particularly difficult for American women to accept their bodies as they are. Acceptance is even harder for women with obvious physical disabilities, since there are constant reminders that they do not measure up to the cultural ideal.

▸ Body image and weight

Although true obesity is associated with certain serious medical conditions (such as hypertension, diabetes, and coronary artery disease), the thinness to which many women aspire has much more to do with fashion than with health. Because of concern about the health effects of overweight, a fear and loathing of body fat (and by extension in some circles, dietary fat) has pervaded certain segments of our society. These feelings probably have more to do with a fear of losing control than with concerns about health.

As a result of our culture's obsession with thinness, both overweight men and overweight women are subjected to job discrimination, name-calling by strangers, and ridicule when they exercise or show signs of sexuality. But overweight women in particular are made to feel as though their weight and their worth as a human being were one and the same.

A recent study from the Harvard School of Public Health and the Harvard School of Medicine showed that obese young adults of both sexes, but particularly women, are less likely to marry than thinner people and can expect to earn less money with the same job qualifications. Overweight women are also subjected to much harsher character judgments than are overweight men and are frequently given unsolicited advice about cultivating their willpower. They are likely to be treated as if they were somehow morally deficient for being overweight.

Afraid of being judged, some of these women only nibble on "acceptable" low-calorie foods when they eat in front of other people, and then make up the difference by eating higher-calorie foods in secret. Because self-esteem is so closely linked to body image in women, overweight women frequently shrink into the background—both literally by slumping and figuratively by keeping quiet and withdrawn. Alternatively, they cultivate a strong wit or self-mocking persona as a defense. They may also develop a number of stress-related disorders (irritable bowel syndrome, headaches, back pain) because of the pressure they feel just getting through each day without being humiliated.

Even women who fall within a normal weight range become obsessed with the bathroom scale. There are perfectly healthy women who cannot get out of bed before they plan precisely what they are going to allow themselves to eat that day, nor can they go from one meal to the next without feeling guilty about every excess calorie they have consumed. This obsession with weight rather than health has led millions of women to develop a pattern of yo-yo (up and down) dieting and, in some cases, eating disorders that can be life-threatening.

▸ Body image in adolescence

The rapid physical changes of puberty make both boys and girls feel self-conscious and awkward about their bodies. In preteen and early adolescent years, girls whose bodies are not maturing "on average" tend to have a particularly negative body image and low self-esteem. The girl who has her growth spurt earlier than her classmates or who starts developing breasts before the others generally feels self-conscious. So does the girl who is shorter or less well developed than her peers.

It is normal for both boys and girls nearing puberty to gain weight just before undergoing the growth spurt, and girls who do not gain sufficient weight and body fat often fail to start menstruating on schedule. Nonetheless, because girls and young women feel they need to be thin, many preteen and adolescent girls go on low-calorie or starvation diets, thus depriving themselves of nutrients essential for normal development.

In middle adolescence (usually the high school years), many girls begin to feel more comfortable with their new body image, but some do not. If a girl feels that her appearance does not correspond to accepted notions of femininity, or if she is confused about her sexual preference, negative feelings about her body may persist. Other members of a teenager's family play an important role in the development of a young woman's body image. Parents who make their daughter feel that she is physically attractive and who accept her newly acquired sexuality can contribute greatly to her self-esteem. Many psychologists argue that encouragement from the father can be particularly important in helping a girl establish a positive sense of herself as a woman. Mothers can also help by providing information about normal physical changes and by serving as a role model of a person comfortable in her own body.

▸ Body image in the reproductive years

For many women pregnancy enhances body image by making them feel that their body is working properly—even if they never before measured up to other physical standards of femininity. These women feel joy as they watch their waistline expand and their breasts swell. For other women the physical changes of pregnancy destroy a positive body image that rested on maintaining a trim waistline, clear skin, and small nipples.

After childbirth some women may have trouble adjusting to their fuller or altered figure or to stretchmarks or to scars left from a cesarean section. Others begin to dislike their body as they struggle to lose the excess pounds gained during pregnancy or discover that leaking milk and engorged breasts make them feel as though they have no control over their own body.

Traumatic events associated with reproduction such as miscarriage, stillbirth, or genetic defects can be devastating to a woman's body image. These events leave some women feeling inadequate in what they consider their most basic biological role. A woman who has had a miscarriage or stillbirth may feel that there is something fundamentally wrong with her body because it cannot carry a healthy pregnancy to term or because it produced a nonviable embryo or fetus. A woman who has conceived a genetically defective child may feel guilty for carrying a genetic disease or feel angry at other women who are pregnant or who have normal children. The associated problems with self-esteem often lead to sexual dysfunction and other marital difficulties.

Many women in their 30s who have postponed having children

discover that they have an infertility problem which precludes their becoming pregnant. Still other women reach their late 30s without finding a partner with whom to have a child. In both of these situations women may begin to develop a negative body image, as they see signs of aging in a body that has not fulfilled its reproductive potential.

Although negative feelings such as these are unwarranted, many women who have reproductive difficulties find that they are haunted by them even as they fight them intellectually. Sometimes it can be useful to talk with a genetic counselor, psychotherapist, or other clinician who can help the woman assess herself more objectively, reduce her sense of grief and guilt, and put this particular problem into the context of her life as a whole. Many women find it helpful to talk with other women (individually or in support groups) who have experienced similar disappointments.

▸ Body image and getting older

Among all women, from full-time homemakers to full-time professionals, we tend to associate sexual attractiveness, particularly female attractiveness, with youth. The result is that many women find it particularly difficult to "grow old gracefully." Women whose self-esteem was once based on conforming to accepted standards of beauty often find they do not know how to behave when people respond to them on another level. It is not uncommon for women nearing or past menopause to try (usually in vain) to rid themselves of the excess weight that comes with age, to dress themselves in garments more suited to a younger woman, to dye their hair, to bury their faces under camouflaging makeup, or to invest in a face lift or tummy tuck.

For some women, these efforts may help maintain a positive body image, if only temporarily. Many other women begin to feel better about their bodies only when they come to accept the inevitable and learn to appreciate—even if not everyone else can—aspects of themselves they may have overlooked earlier in life.

Seeking Help

Psychotherapy

Psychotherapy is a form of treatment for psychological and emotional disorders that involves communication—through words and behavior—between a psychotherapist and a patient. Although there are dozens of forms of psychotherapy, some of which have overlapping philosophies, they can be divided into two basic kinds: psychodynamic and behavioral. Depending on the disorder, therapists may combine aspects of both approaches in treatment.

▸ Psychodynamic therapies

Psychodynamic therapies are forms of "talk therapy" in which the psychotherapist and patient together attempt to uncover emotions and motivations assumed to underlie a psychological or emotional disorder. The aim is to connect the patient's internal experience with her responses to life events—all in a safe, therapeutic setting—and then to use this new understanding to bring about positive changes in these responses. Conflicts often stem from early childhood events or relationships with parents.

Psychodynamic therapy may continue for an indefinite period of time. Although it may involve a one-to-one relationship between therapist and patient, as in individual therapy, its principles are also used in many forms of group therapy, including some family and couples therapy and self-help/support groups (which may, but do not necessarily, include a psychotherapist as facilitator).

Psychoanalysis is a highly specialized form of psychodynamic therapy based in the work of Sigmund Freud and his successors, who have extended and modified his ideas. Freud theorized that psychological problems could be alleviated by putting traumatic memories and emotions into words. Some therapists still practice classical psychoanalysis, which delves into the patient's unconscious thought and past experience to achieve a major deconstruction and reconstruction of the personality. The trend today, how-

213

ever, is toward using psychoanalytic techniques less stringently to uncover insights into the patient's current life situation. To be effective, this form of psychotherapy often requires long hours of work over many years and can be quite costly.

▸ Behavioral therapies

In contrast to psychoanalysis and other psychodynamic forms of psychotherapy, behavioral therapies are concerned with the problem behavior itself rather than its psychological roots in the past or the unconscious. Using specific techniques from learning theory (such as classical conditioning, which originated in Ivan Pavlov's research on dogs), the behavioral therapist helps people learn to change undesirable responses (either actions or feelings) to a particular situation or stimulus.

A behavioral therapy such as systematic desensitization, for example, can help people overcome phobias or panic disorder through repeated and deliberate exposure to whatever stimulus provokes the symptoms. Over time the person learns to substitute feelings of relaxation for feelings of fear or anxiety. Similarly, in assertiveness training a person learns to substitute clear and direct expressions of anger for feelings of anxiety or fear.

Other types of behavioral therapy include training in social skills such as listening and starting a conversation, and biofeedback, which is used to treat stress-related conditions such as headache (see Alternative Therapies) and to manage anxiety. Sex therapy (see Sexual Dysfunction) also relies on techniques of behavioral psychotherapy in addressing a particular couple's needs.

Cognitive therapy, a major form of behavior therapy, is premised on the belief that negative or distorted patterns of thinking underlie various psychological problems. A depressed woman, for example, may consider herself worthless, and consistently interpret other people's responses as negative and judgmental—a pattern of thinking that becomes a self-perpetuating cycle of self-denigration. After helping to identify such patterns, the therapist guides the patient in adopting more functional alternatives.

▸ Feminist therapy

Practitioners of more mainstream psychotherapy—regardless of whether their basic approach is psychodynamic, behavioral, or both—frequently incorporate principles of what is called feminist therapy into their practice. These principles include the idea that the therapist is not the healer but rather the facilitator of the woman's recovery, that the woman is a client rather than a patient, that the woman has the means of recovery within herself, and that women in general are not only active and independent in their own right but are equal to, if in many ways different from, men.

It is the centrality of these feminist ideas that characterizes a feminist therapy or therapist. In addition, for feminist therapists, societal and cultural conflicts are just as important—if not more so—as internal conflicts as the sources of women's psychological problems. It is not surprising, then, that feminist therapists were pioneers in recognizing the relationship between psychological problems such as depression, anxiety, and personality disorders and events in a woman's past such as domestic abuse, rape, incest, or alcohol and substance abuse. For example, a major focus of feminist therapy with a lesbian client would be to acknowledge how damaging it is to live in a homophobic society, rather than to explore the origins of the woman's sexual preferences.

▸ Finding a psychotherapist

Psychotherapy can be a tremendous help in treating many psychological and emotional disorders, but practiced improperly, it can result in tremendous harm. For this reason it is important to select a psychotherapist with care. Not only should the person chosen have training and experience appropriate for treating the particular disorder, but also patient and therapist should have compatible styles and values. In fact, the rapport between patient and therapist is often much more essential to success than is the therapist's specific philosophy.

This is not to say that a person seeking a psychotherapist should not learn as much as possible about a potential therapist's philosophy, approach, and training, as well as about the cost of each session and whether it is covered by insurance. The therapist should be asked to estimate how long therapy will continue (months or years) and to set up a specific timetable for evaluating progress. Response varies so much from patient to patient, however, that it is unreasonable to expect a therapist to predict exactly how many sessions will be required.

Because today's managed care health programs restrict most patients' access to long-term therapy, goals and realistic short-term expectations need to be established at the outset. In recent years short-term behavioral therapy has been found to be effective in treating clinical depression, anxiety, and phobias, as well as other immediate areas of emotional conflict. The success of any therapy depends on the patient's basic motivation, her willingness to mobilize her own resources, and the degree of trust and esteem that exists between her and her therapist.

It is also worth thinking about which type of psychotherapist is appropriate for treating a given psychological disorder. A great deal of confusion exists about the differences between the many types of specialists who practice psychotherapy. Many people, for example, confuse psychiatrists, psychologists, and psychoanalysts.

- Psychiatrists are physicians who have undergone 4 years of medical school as well as 4 years of a psychiatric residency, which includes training in psychotherapy. They are the only psychotherapists who can prescribe drugs or perform physical examinations.
- Licensed psychologists have specialized training (usually a doctorate) in treating emotional problems, performing psychological tests, and practicing psychotherapy.
- Psychoanalysts (who can be either psychiatrists or psychologists) also have additional training in the practice of psychoanalysis.

Among the many other specialists who may practice psychotherapy are psychiatric nurses, MSWs (people holding a master's degree in social work), other social workers, marriage and family counselors, ministers, rabbis, priests, and other members of the clergy, as well as individuals trained in specific approaches such as Gestalt therapy, transactional analysis, family therapy, couples counseling, and Jungian psychoanalysis. The training, experience, and philosophy of these disciplines varies greatly.

Interviewing therapists to evaluate their training and philosophy can seem overwhelming, but few people have to do it on their own. Most of the time a short list of eligible psychotherapists can be garnered from friends, clinicians, school counselors, community health centers, or support groups. Women's health clinics and feminist organizations may also be able to provide names of feminist therapists.

▸ Choosing the treatment setting

A careful initial diagnostic assessment of a patient's situation is necessary before she and a therapist can determine together which approach and which therapeutic setting will be most appropriate and effective. These decisions influence how active a role the therapist will play in the therapeutic relationship—or alliance—with the patient and whether treatment will take place in an individual or a group setting.

Individual therapy, a one-to-one interaction between therapist and patient, is a familiar model, but a group structure has also proven helpful in many instances and is sometimes the only form of treatment available or the only one covered by an individual's health insurance. The goal of group therapy is to offer a context that encourages group members to work on underlying conflicts and move toward a more autonomous self through mutual support and interaction. Issues such as inclusion and acceptance, power and independence, and equality and sharing characterize the group's evolution. Group therapy may involve one therapist and a number of patients, or several therapists and large or small groups.

Family therapy—a variation on group therapy which has emerged over the last several decades—focuses on the individual's problems within the context of family dynamics. The therapist meets with the patient—a woman with anorexia, for example—and other family members to probe long-established patterns of interaction and role playing. These may have served to maintain the emotional and psychological equilibrium of the family unit, but at the expense of the individual family member. Without taking sides, the therapist seeks to clarify family interactions in order to open up channels of communication and create a space for movement and growth.

Couples therapy, another form of family intervention, addresses problems in interactions between partners. Understanding that their negative exchanges are mutually reinforcing helps couples clarify their difficulties and begin to resolve them through improved communication.

Psychodrama, or group dramatization of situations that embody underlying conflicts, feelings, and tensions, is a useful approach for those who have difficulty expressing themselves in words. Through their actions, patients bring to awareness and express those parts of themselves they cannot talk about directly.

It can take a fair amount of time (and sometimes money) to choose a compatible therapist and an appropriate treatment setting. It may be necessary for a person to meet with several candidates before she finds one with the right style. Ultimately, it is up to the patient to decide within the first two or three sessions if things feel right. This can be particularly difficult for someone living with emotional pain at the same time. Still, leaving the decision about compatibility up to the therapist is, in the end, counterproductive.

Alternative Therapies

In recent years millions of Americans have turned to acupuncture, biofeedback, visualization, and crystal healing as alternatives to conventional therapy, or have "mixed and matched" conventional therapy with other, seemingly incompatible healing options. The highest use of alternative approaches is reported by relatively well educated and affluent whites from 25 to 49 years of age.

Many physicians question the more extravagant claims of alternative therapies. They warn that these practices, if not downright dangerous in their own right, may keep people from seeking effective treatment. But it is becoming harder to deny that at least *some* alternative techniques work for *some* patients—even if medical science cannot explain exactly how.

Hands-on therapies. Acupuncture, a hands-on therapy, is gaining acceptance in many circles. Still regarded as an alternative practice in the United States, it has been a conventional therapy in China for thousands of years. Acupuncturists contend that the body consists of a system of specific "vital energy" or "life force" (called *qi* or *chi*) pathways. Disease and pain result when the energy flow of these pathways is interrupted. Acupuncturists say they can rebalance the flow by inserting hair-thin needles into precise points along the pathways and then manipulating them.

Particularly impressive to many Western researchers is acupuncture's effectiveness as a pain reliever. Western science has yet to explain how this works. The most convincing hypothesis so far is that the puncture somehow stimulates nerve cells to produce chemicals called endorphins, the body's natural painkillers. A few animal studies have shown that inhibiting the release of these chemicals can block acupuncture's anesthetic effect. In other studies animals became partially anesthetized after being injected with body fluids from other animals that had undergone acupuncture. Whatever the explanation, recent reports in esteemed medical journals indicate that acupuncture can relieve chronic back pain, as well as the pain of osteoarthritis and rheumatoid arthritis. It is also used as a surgical anesthetic and to relieve withdrawal symptoms in recovering alcoholics, drug addicts, and cigarette smokers.

In acupressure the same energy points cited by acupuncturists are massaged with finger pressure, primarily to relieve stress. Shiatsu is the Japanese equivalent of this technique. Similarly, practitioners of therapeutic touch claim to unblock energy flow by moving their hands over a patient's "energy fields." Proponents insist that this technique not only improves overall well-being but also relieves pain and anxiety and even speeds wound healing.

Reflexology is yet another massage technique based on Eastern teachings, this time with emphasis on the feet. Reflexologists have mapped specific areas of the sole to every organ, gland, and body part. The heel corresponds to the lower body, the middle of the sole to the digestive organs, the ball of the foot to heart and lungs, and the toes to the head. By stimulating relevant points, reflexologists claim to be able to relieve pain and stress and improve circulation in corresponding areas of the body. Most conventional doctors are skeptical of this technique, suggesting that self-massage, Epsom salt baths, and foot exercises provide equivalent health benefits.

Even without an elaborate map of energy pathways, alternative healers use other massage techniques to relieve stress and discomfort. "Hellerwork," for example, involves numerous 1½-hour deep-massage sessions on the theory that pain and tension in body structures increase risk of injury. To ease stress, depression, tension headaches, exhaustion, and various other woes, the "Alexander technique" teaches patients how to improve posture in a dozen or so sessions. Conventional practitioners generally question the more grandiose benefits attributed to such practices, but many acknowledge that at the very least these techniques may relieve stress simply because the therapist is paying attention to the patient.

Mind–body techniques. Alternative practices based on the influence of mind over body have been entering the mainstream lately, partly because of recent discoveries in a new field called psychoneuroimmunology. Researchers in this field explore the way behavior and emotions influence the nervous and immune system, and their findings are starting to close the mind–body gap that so bothers critics of modern Western science. For example, research at Stanford University showed that women with advanced breast cancer receiving standard therapy live twice as long if they also participate in a support group.

Psychoneuroimmunology could potentially provide scientific evidence for a belief held by healers, both mainstream and alternative, from the earliest days of medicine: that healing the mind is an integral part of healing the body. The evidence gleaned so far has not convinced medical scientists that mental states can actually cause, cure, or prevent diseases. But this type of research does open new possibilities for easing the discomfort of disease, surgery, or chemotherapy.

Biofeedback is a particularly popular mind–body technique. Through it, patients learn how to regulate their ordinarily involuntary body functions such as heart rate, temperature, and muscle tension. Hooked up to machines that measure these functions, patients watch a display or listen to a tone that tells them how close their physiological responses are getting to a desired result. Eventually they learn to control responses without feedback from the machine. After ruling out physical problems, many conventional doctors now use biofeedback to treat pain and anxiety, migraine or tension headaches, and chronic pain syndrome. Many private insurers are willing to pay for biofeedback training sessions.

Another mind–body technique increasingly used by mainstream physicians is hypnosis—even though, as with biofeedback, understanding of the physical mechanism or even hard evidence of effectiveness remains limited. Once regarded as sheer chicanery, hypnotherapy is now practiced by thousands of medical doctors in conjunction with conventional medical techniques. It can be used to help patients break bad habits, overcome phobias and sexual dysfunction, and cope with pain. Therapists help patients go into a trancelike state in which they lose awareness of their body and become more responsive to suggestion. When the session ends, patients remember everything that happened.

The American Medical Association's Council on Scientific Affairs has called for more research into hypnotherapy to help elucidate its role and means of action. Some practitioners hypothesize that hypnotherapy stimulates the brain's limbic system, which has been linked to emotions and normally involuntary activities such as digestion and hormone regulation. This link may explain in part the observation that hypnotherapy has helped control the stomach acid secretions of ulcer patients, reduce the discomfort of chemotherapy, and even speed recovery from burns.

Other mind–body techniques aim at reducing stress, a poorly defined concept that has been linked repeatedly to a series of ailments. Therapists at the Harvard-affiliated Mind/Body Medical Institute in Boston teach relaxation techniques such as meditation and yoga to help relieve stress in patients with coronary artery disease, infertility, insomnia, chronic pain, AIDS, and cancer. Other medical centers around the country have established their own meditation or massage clinics or have simply begun to emphasize listening and touching as crucial aspects of treatment. And stress-reduction techniques such as meditation and yoga are now often taught to patients by conventional health care workers, most commonly nurses, psychologists, and social workers, to help them face pain more effectively, including the pain of labor and childbirth. How, or if, they influence the course of any given disease is not known.

Even less conventional are New Age relaxation devices such as flotation tanks and isolation chambers, which separate patients from all environmental stimuli. The same can be said for bioenergetics, in which the therapist passes an invisible and unmeasurable "energy" to the patient. In crystal healing energized light is supposedly passed through quartz or other colored minerals. Some patients claim to relax with the help of a "synchroenergizer," which surrounds them with New Age music and pulsing lights. For all these practices, evidence of any therapeutic effect that satisfies the standards of conventional medicine is lacking, and consumers are wise to be skeptical.

Visualization (guided imagery) is a relaxation technique which involves learning to picture each muscle relaxing. Introduced in the 1970s to improve the performance of athletes and musicians, visualization is also used to promote healing. Therapists teach patients to imagine their body righting a biochemical imbalance or conquering microorganisms. Although evidence for successful cures remains largely anecdotal, many hospitals and private psychologists have ongoing visualization groups for patients battling serious illness.

Because alternative therapies do not rely on the same standards of proof as conventional medicine, it is often difficult to distinguish a potentially effective therapy from a pure hoax. Still, common sense can be a fairly reliable guide. Anyone seeking alternative care should avoid healers who claim to cure everything, those who offer "too good to be true" cures for serious diseases such as AIDS and cancer, and those who require multiple visits at hefty rates. Furthermore, some forms of alternative therapy have already entered the mainstream of medicine, at least for a well-defined set of conditions. Awareness of these differences can help anyone trying to choose from the many options.

Additional evidence for and against alternative practices may come from studies funded by a new Office of Alternative Medicine at the National Institutes of Health, long a champion of rigorous scientific medicine. Created in 1992, this bureau administers grants to researchers who plan to evaluate the claims of alternative therapies using the same methods and standards of reproducibility required of more conventional practices. Many health care workers hope that these studies will reveal new ways of dealing with some currently intractable problems in both the mental and physical health of women.

For More Information

The following resources are not intended to be exhaustive but to indicate possible starting points for any woman seeking more information on a given topic than this *Guide* provides. Most entries cite one or two books with up-to-date information and, when available, the names and addresses of organizations that provide reliable information and patient support. When appropriate, other resources, such as audiotapes, videotapes, software, and Internet sites and newsgroups, are listed.

Where to Look. Organizations usually are listed once, under the most inclusive entry.

Books. Most titles cited are in print and available through booksellers. The exceptions should be in the collections of most libraries.

Organizations. Addresses may have changed since the book went to press. The initial "1" has been dropped from all telephone numbers, since most areas of the country now have to dial 1 before long-distance calls.

Electronic resources. Resources are listed for the Internet and World Wide Web only. Also worth exploring are information and support groups available through commercial online services, such as America Online, CompuServe, and Prodigy. Accessing information on the World Wide Web requires an Internet connection and browser software, such as Netscape or Mosaic. Most Web addresses carry the standard prefix *http://*. Subscriptions to mailing lists also require e-mail capability, either through a direct Internet connection or a commercial online service. Readers who would like a general introduction to finding resources on the Internet can consult:

Daniel P. Dern, *The Internet Guide for New Users* (New York: McGraw-Hill, 1994).

Matthew Naythons et al., *The Internet Health, Fitness, and Medicine Yellow Pages* (New York: McGraw Hill, 1995).

Douglas Goldstein and Joyce Flory, *The Online Consmer Guide to Health Care and Wellness* (np: Irwin Professional Publications, 1996).

Michael Wolff, ed., *Netdoctor: Your Guide to Health and Medical Advice on the Internet* (np: Wolff New Media, 1996).

General resources

National Women's Health Resource Center
Suite 325
2440 M St. N.W.
Washington, DC 20037
202-293-6045
Publication: Bimonthly health update

National Black Women's Health Project (NBWHP)
1237 Ralph David Abernathy Blvd., S.W.
Atlanta, GA 30310
800-ASK-BWHP (800-275-2947)

National Institute on Aging
P.O. Box 8057
Gaithersburg, MD 20898-8057
800-222-2225

National Latina Health Organization (NLHO)
P.O. Box 7567
Oakland, CA 94601
510-534-1362

National Women's Health Network (NWHN)
514 10th Street NW
Washington, DC 20004
202-347-1140

Native American Women's Health Education Resource Center
P.O. Box 572
Lake Andes, SD 57356
605-487-7072
Fax 605-487-7964

Women of All Red Nations (WARN)
4511 N. Hermitage
Chicago, IL 60640

Women of Color Partnership Program
Religious Coalition for Abortion Rights
1025 Vermont NW
Suite 1130
Washington, DC 20005
202-628-7700
Publication: *Common Ground, Different Planes*, newsletter on reproductive health issues for women of color.

Harvard Women's Health Watch
Harvard Medical School Health Publications Group
164 Longwood Avenue
Boston, MA 02115-5818
617-432-1485
A monthly newsletter that explores health topics unique to women.

Harvard Mental Health Letter
Harvard Medical School Health Publications Group
164 Longwood Avenue
Boston, MA 02115-5818
617-432-1485
A monthly newsletter that addresses current mental health issues.

Women's Health Forum
6113 Abbey Road
Aptos, CA 95003
408-662-8500
Fax: 408-662-1826
An interdisciplinary newsletter on health topics of interest to women.

The Black Women's Health Book: Speaking for Ourselves (Seattle: Seal Press,
    1994).

Depression in Women

National Institute of Mental Health
5600 Fishers Lane
Rockville, MD 20857
Hotline: 800-421-4211
Pamphlet: "Depression: What Every Woman Should Know."

Depressives Anonymous: Recovery from Depression
329 E. 62nd St.
New York, NY 10021
212-689-2600

On the Internet: Two online mailing lists for people with mood disorders: Pendulum, for people diagnosed with manic depression and other bipolar disorders, and Walkers in Darkness, for people diagnosed with various depressive disorders. To subscribe to either list, send a message to majordomo@ncar.ucar.edu containing the line "subscribe pendulum" or "subscribe walkers."

Dana Crowley Jack, *Silencing the Self: Women and Depression* (Cambridge, MA: Harvard University Press, 1991).

Ellen McGrath, *Getting Up When You're Feeling Low: A Woman's Guide to Overcoming and Preventing Depression* (New York: Putnam, 1988).

Maggie Scarf, *Unfinished Business: Pressure Points in the Lives of Women* (New York: Ballantine, 1991).

Antidepressants

The PDR Family Guide to Women's Health and Prescription Drugs (Montvale, NJ: Medical Economics Data, 1993).

Peter Kramer, *Listening to Prozac: A Psychiatrist Explores Anti-Depressant Drugs and the Remaking of the Self* (New York: Viking Penguin, 1994).

Seasonal Affective Disorder

National Organization for Seasonal Affective Disorder (NOSAD)
P.O. Box 40133
Washington, DC 20016
Publications: Newsletter and information packet.

On the Internet: A newsgroup, alt.support.depression.seasonal, provides an online meeting place for people with SAD to share information.

Norman E. Rosenthal, *Winter Blues: Seasonal Affective Disorder* (New York: Guilford Press, 1994).

Manic-Depressive Disorder

National Depressive and Manic Depressive Association
Suite 501
730 N. Franklin St.
Chicago, IL 60610
312-642-0049

Lithium Information Center
Dean Foundation
Suite 302
8000 Excelsior Dr.
Madison, WI 53717-1914
608-836-8070

National Foundation for Depressive Illness
5th Floor
245 Seventh Ave.
New York, NY 10001
212-620-7637
800-248-4344

On the Internet: An online mailing list, Pendulum, provides a forum for people diagnosed with manic depression and other bipolar disorders. To subscribe, send a message to majordomo@ncar.ucar.edu containing the line "subscribe pendulum." There is also a newsgroup, alt.support.depression.manic.

Patty Duke Astin, *A Brilliant Madness: Living with Manic-Depressive Illness* (New York: Bantam, 1992).

Diane Berger and Lisa Berger, *We Heard the Angels of Madness: One Family's Struggle with Manic Depression* (New York: Morrow, 1992).

F. K. Goodwin and K. R. Jamison, *Manic-Depressive Illness* (New York and Oxford: Oxford University Press, 1990).

Kay Redfield, *An Unquiet Mind* (New York: Knopf, 1995).

Anxiety in Women

Anxiety Disorders Association of America
Suite 513
6000 Executive Blvd.
Rockville, MD 20852
301-231-9350

On the Internet: A newsgroup, alt.support.anxiety-panic, provides a place for people with anxiety disorders to share experiences with others.

Mark S. Gold, *The Good News about Panic, Anxiety, and Phobias* (New York: Bantam, 1990).

Jerilyn Ross, *Triumph over Fear: A Book of Help and Hope for People with Anxiety, Panic Attacks, and Phobias* (New York: Bantam, 1994).

Panic Disorder

Anxiety Disorders Association of America
Suite 513
6000 Executive Blvd.
Rockville, MD 20852
301-231-9350

National Anxiety Foundation
3135 Custer Drive
Lexington, KY 40517-4001

National Institute of Mental Health
Panic Campaign
Room 15C-05
5600 Fishers Lane
Rockville, MD 20857

On the Internet: A newsgroup, alt.support.anxiety-panic, provides a place for people with panic disorders to share experiences with others.

M. S. Gold, *The Good News about Panic, Anxiety, and Phobias* (New York: Bantam, 1989).

Jerilyn Ross, *Triumph over Fear: A Book of Help and Hope for People with Anxiety, Panic Attacks, and Phobias* (New York, Bantam, 1994).

Obsessive-Compulsive Disorder

Obsessive Compulsive Foundation
P.O. Box 70
Milford, CT 06460
203-878-5669

Judith L. Rapoport, *The Boy Who Couldn't Stop Washing* (New York: Signet, 1989).

Posttraumatic Stress Disorder

Judith Lewis Herman, *Trauma and Recovery: The Aftermath of Violence: From Domestic Abuse to Political Terror* (New York: Basic Books, 1992).

Antianxiety Drugs

The PDR Family Guide to Women's Health and Prescription Drugs (Montvale, NJ: Medical Economics Data, 1993).

Anorexia and Bulimia

American Anorexic/Bulimia Association (AA/BA)
Suite 1 R
293 Central Park West
New York, NY 10024
212-501-8351

Anorexia Nervosa and Related Eating Disorders
P.O. Box 5102
Eugene, OR 97405
503-344-1144

National Association of Anorexia Nervosa and
Associated Disorders
P.O. Box 7
Highland Park, IL 60035
847-831-3438

Katherine Byrne, *A Parent's Guide to Anorexia and Bulimia: Understanding and Helping Self-Starvers and Binge/Purgers* (New York: Schocken Books, 1987).

James Moorey, *Living with Anorexia and Bulimia* (New York: St. Martin's, 1991).

Kathleen Zraly and David Swift, *Overcoming Eating Disorders: Recovery from Anorexia, Bulimia, and Compulsive Overeating* (New York: Crossroad Publishing, 1992).

Psychosomatic Disorders

American Chronic Pain Association
257 Old Haymaker Rd.
Monroeville, PA 15146
412-856-9676

National Chronic Pain Outreach Association
7979 Old Georgetown Road
Suite 100
Bethesda, MD 20814
301-652-4948

Susan Baur, *Hypochondria: Woeful Imaginations* (Berkeley: University of California Press, 1988).

Edward Shorter, *From the Mind into the Body: The Cultural Origins of Psychosomatic Symptoms* (New York: Free Press, 1994).

Phillip R. Slavney, *Perspectives on "Hysteria"* (Baltimore: The Johns Hopkins University Press, 1990).

Postpartum Psychiatric Disorders

Depression after Delivery
P.O. Box 1282
Morrisville, PA 19067
215-295-3994

Carol Dix, *The New Mother Syndrome* (New York: Doubleday & Company, 1985).

Karen P. Kleima and Valerie D. Raskin, *This Isn't What I Expected: Recognizing and Recovering from Depression and Anxiety after Childbirth* (New York: Bantam, 1994).

Schizophrenia

The National Alliance for the Mentally Ill
Suite 1015
200 North Glebe Rd.
Arlington, VA 22203-3754
703-524-7600

National Mental Health Association
1021 Prince St.
Alexandria, VA 22314-2971
703-684-7722

The National Mental Health Consumers' Association
Suite 1100
1211 Chestnut St.
Philadelphia, PA 19107
215-735-2465

Center for Psychiatric Rehabilitation
Boston University
930 Commonwealth Avenue
Boston, MA 02215
617-353-3549
A resource center for information about chronic mental illness.

On the Internet: A newsgroup, alt.support.schizophrenia, provides an on-line meeting place for people with this illness to share information.

Richard S. E. Keefe and Phillip D. Harvey, *Understanding Schizophrenia: A Guide to the New Research on Causes and Treatment* (New York: Free Press, 1994).

Alzheimer's Disease

Alzheimer's Association
Suite 1000
919 North Michigan Ave.
Chicago, IL 60611-1676
312-335-8700
800-272-3900
Call the local chapter to see if it sponsors a support group for people with early-stage Alzheimer's.

On the Internet: On the World Wide Web, the Alzheimer's Association at http://www.alz.org provides information on 200 local chapters, a fact sheet on the disease, on-line brochures for caregivers, and information on the latest drugs and treatments.

Miriam K. Aronson, ed., *Understanding Alzheimer's Disease* (New York: Scribner's, 1988).

Howard Gruetzner, *Alzheimer's: A Caregiver's Guide and Sourcebook* (New York: Wiley, 1992).

Rose Oliver and Frances A. Bock, *Coping with Alzheimer's: A Caregiver's Emotional Survival Guide* (North Hollywood, CA: Wilshire, 1989).

Domestic Abuse

National Coalition against Domestic Violence
P.O. Box 18749
Denver, CO 80218
303-839-1852

On the Internet: SafetyNet, a list of domestic violence resources with links to other net sites, is located at http://www.pmedia.com/cy-bergrrl/dv.html.

Robert J. Ackerman and Susan E. Pickering, *Abused No More: Recovery for Women from Abusive or Co-Dependent Relationships* (New York: Sulzburger & Graham, 1989).

Judith Lewis Herman, *Trauma and Recovery: The Aftermath of Violence* (New York: Basic Books, 1993).

Sexual Harassment

9 to 5
The National Association of Working Women
Suite 205
145 Tremont Street
Boston, MA 02111
800-522-0925

Ellen Bravo and Ellen Cassedy, *The 9 to 5 Guide to Combating Sexual Harassment: Candid Advice from 9 to 5, the National Association of Working Women* (New York: Wiley, 1992).

Celia Morris, *Bearing Witness: Sexual Harassment and Beyond—Everywoman's Story* (Boston: Little, Brown, 1994).

William Petrocelli and Barbara Kate Repa, *Sexual Harassment on the Job* (Berkeley, CA: Nolo Press, 1992).

Rape

National Coalition against Sexual Assault (NCASA)
P.O. Box 21378
Washington, DC 20009
202-483-7165

Women against Rape (WAR)
Box 02084
Columbus, OH 43202
614-291-9751

Sponsors rape-prevention training, including self-defense, in addition to support groups for rape survivors.

National Clearinghouse on Marital and Date Rape (NCOMDR)
Women's History Research, Inc.
2325 Oak Street
Berkeley, CA 94708
415-524-1582

Pauline Bart and Patricia O'Brien, *Stopping Rape: Successful Survival Strategies* (Elmsford, NY: Pergamon Press, 1985).

Susan Estrich, *Real Rape* (Cambridge, MA: Harvard University Press, 1987).

Migael Scherer, *Still Loved by the Sun: A Rape Survivor's Journal* (New York: NAL-Dutton, 1993).

Robin Warshaw, *I Never Called It Rape: The Ms. Report on Recognizing, Fighting and Surviving Date and Acquaintance Rape* (New York: Harper & Row, 1988).

Sexual Abuse and Incest

Ellen Bass and Laura Davis, *The Courage to Heal: A Guide for Women Survivors of Child Sexual Abuse* (New York: HarperCollins, 1994).

Laura Davis, *Allies in Healing: When the Person You Love Was Sexually Abused as a Child* (New York: HarperCollins, 1991).

Judith Lewis Herman, *Father-Daughter Incest* (Cambridge: Harvard University Press, 1981).

Wendy Maltz and Beverly Holman, *Incest and Sexuality: A Guide to Understanding and Healing* (Lexington, MA: D. C. Heath, 1987).

Sexual Response

D. Bullard and S. Knight, *Sexuality and Disability, Personal Perspectives* (St. Louis: Mosby, 1981).

Robert N. Butler and Myrna I. Lewis, *Midlife Love Life* (New York: Perennial Library, 1988).

Terence T. Gorski, *Getting Love Right: Learning the Choices of Healthy Intimacy* (New York: Simon & Schuster, 1993).

Matthew McKay et al., *Couple Skills: Making Your Relationship Work* (Oakland, CA: New Harbinger, 1994).

Sexual Preference

Margaret Cruikshank, ed., *The Lesbian Path: Women Loving Women* (San Francisco: Grey Fox, 1985).

Lillian Faderman, *Odd Girls and Twilight Lovers: A History of Lesbian Life in Twentieth-Century America* (New York: Columbia University Press, 1991).

April Martin, *Lesbian and Gay Parenting Handbook: Creating and Raising Our Families* (New York: HarperCollins, 1993).

C. M. Renzetti, *Violent Betrayal: Lesbian Partner Abuse* (Newbury Park: Sage Publications, 1992).

Sexual Dysfunction

American Association of Sex Educators, Counselors, Therapists
Suite 1717
435 N. Michigan Ave.
Chicago, IL 60611
312-644-0828

L. G. Barbach, *For Yourself: The Fulfillment of Female Sexuality* (New York: Doubleday, 1981).

Julia Heiman, *Becoming Orgasmic* (New York: Simon & Schuster, 1987).

Linda Valins, *When a Woman's Body Says No to Sex: Understanding and Overcoming Vaginismus* (New York: Viking, 1992).

Stress

American Institute of Stress
124 Park Ave.
Yonkers, NY 10703
914-963-1200
800-24-RELAX (800-247-3529)
Publication: Newsletter; call for free sample.

Audiovision
3 Morningside Pl.
Norwalk, CT 06854
800-367-1604
Publication: Catalogue of books and audio and video tapes on managing stress, including "A Day Away from Stress" (available as audio or
video), a combination of breathing exercises, guided imagery, music,
and environmental sounds.

Harriet B. Braiker, *The Type E Woman: How to Overcome the Stress of Being
Everything to Everybody* (New York: Signet, 1986).

David Elkind, *Ties That Stress: The New Family Imbalance* (Cambridge,
MA: Harvard University Press, 1994).

Arlie Hochschild and Anne Machung, *Second Shift* (New York: Avon,
1990).

Bonita C. Long and Sharon E. Kahn, *Women, Work, and Coping: A Multidisciplinary Approach to Workplace Stress* (Cheektowaga, NY: University of Toronto Press, 1993).

J. Robin Powell and Holly George-Warren, *The Working Woman's Guide
to Managing Stress* (Needham Heights, MA: Prentice Hall School,
1994).

Juliet B. Schor, *The Overworked American: The Unexpected Decline of Lei-
sure* (New York: Basic Books, 1993).

Premenstrual Syndrome

Katharina Dalton, *Once a Month: The Original Premenstrual Syndrome
Handbook* (Alameda, CA: Hunter House, 1990).

Menopause

MidLife Women's Network
5129 Logan Ave. S.
Minneapolis, MN 55419
800-886-4354
Publication: A newsletter, *MidLife Woman*, "designed to inform and empower women who want to improve their health and lives during the midlife years."

Menopause News
Suite 10
2074 Union St.
San Francisco, CA 94123
800-241-MENO (800-241-6366)
A newsletter that aims to provide "an in-depth view of the physical, emotional, and spiritual aspects of menopause."

National Action Forum for Midlife and Older Women
P.O. Box 816
Stony Brook, NY 11790
Publication: *Hot Flash*.

On the Internet: A discussion list, Menopaus, provides a forum where women can discuss menopause-related concerns and share remedies and solutions for common symptoms and problems. To subscribe, send the message "subscribe MENOPAUS <lastname, firstname>" (note that the final "e" in "menopause" should be left off) to listserv@psuhmc.hmc.psu.edu.

Sheldon H. Cherry, *The Menopause Book: A Guide to Health and Well-Being for Women after 40* (New York: Macmillan, 1994).

Lois Jovanovic-Peterson, *A Woman Doctor's Guide to Menopause: Essential Facts and Up-To-The-Minute Information for a Woman's Change of Life* (New York: Hyperion, 1993).

Carol Landau et al., *The Complete Book of Menopause: Every Woman's Guide to Good Health* (New York: G. P. Putnam's Sons, 1994).

Lila Nachtigall and Joan R. Heilman, *Estrogen: A Complete Guide to Reversing the Effects of Menopause Using Hormone Replacement Therapy* (New York: HarperCollins, 1991).

Morris Notelovitz, *Estrogen: Yes or No?* (New York: St. Martin's Press, 1993).

Gayle Sand, *Is It Hot in Here or Is It Me? Facts, Fallacies, and Feelings about Menopause* (New York: HarperCollins, 1993).

Postpartum Emotions

Postpartum Support International
927 N. Kellogg Ave.
Santa Barbara, CA 93111
805-967-7636

The Family Resource Coalition
16th Floor
200 S. Michigan Ave.
Chicago, IL 60604
312-341-0900

On the Internet: A newsgroup, FamilyWeb, provides new parents with a forum to discuss a wide range of infant-care and childrearing issues with other parents.

Elisabeth Bing and Libby Colman, *Losing Weight after Pregnancy: A Step-by-Step Guide to Postpartum Fitness* (New York: Hyperion, 1994).

Ann Dunnewold and Diane G. Sanford, *Postpartum Survival Guide* (Oakland, CA: New Harbinger, 1994).

Sally Placksin, *Mothering the New Mother: Your Postpartum Resource Companion* (New York: Newmarket, 1993).

Insomnia

National Sleep Foundation
Third Floor, PN
122 S. Robertson Blvd.
Los Angeles, CA 90048
800-SHUTEYE (800-748-8393)

On the Internet: A newsgroup, alt.support.sleep-disorder, provides an on-line meeting place for people with sleep disorders to share experiences and information.

Lydia Dotto, *Losing Sleep: How Your Sleeping Habits Affect Your Life* (New York: Morrow, 1992).

Peter Hauri and Shirley Linde, *No More Sleepless Nights: The Complete Program for Ending Insomnia* (New York: Wiley, 1991).

Rebecca Huntley, *Sleep Book for Tired Parents: A Practical Guide to Solving Children's Sleep Problems* (Seattle: Parenting Press, 1993).

Ralph A. Pascauly and Sally Warren Soest, *Snoring and Sleep Apnea: Personal and Family Guide to Diagnosis and Treatment* (New York: Raven Press, 1994).

Alcohol Addiction

American Council for Drug Education
136 E. 64th St.
New York, NY 10021
800-488-DRUG (800-488-3784)

National Clearinghouse for Alcohol and Drug Information
P.O. Box 2345
Rockville, MD 20847-2345
301-468-2600
800-729-6686

Alcoholics Anonymous
P.O. Box 459 Grand Central Station
New York, NY 10163
212-870-3400
Meetings: Consult phonebook for local chapter.

Children of Alcoholics Foundation
P.O. Box 4185
Grand Central Station
New York, NY 10163-4185
212-754-0656
800-359-2623

American Cleft Palate-Craniofacial Association
1218 Grandview Ave.
Pittsburgh, PA 15211
412-481-1376
800-24-CLEFT (800-242-5338)
Provides information about fetal alcohol syndrome.

M. Ellen Stammer, *Women and Alcohol: The Journey Back* (New York: Gardner Press, 1991).

George E. Valliant, *The Natural History of Alcoholism, Revisited* (Cambridge, MA: Harvard University Press, 1995).

Substance Abuse

National Clearinghouse for Alcohol and Drug Information
P.O. Box 2345
Rockville, MD 20847-2345
800-729-6686

US Department of Health and Human Services
800-662-HELP (800-662-4357), information hotline providing drug-specific counseling for addictions

Women's Recovery Programs: A Directory of Residential Addiction Treatment Centers (Phoenix, AZ: Oryx Press, 1990).

Body Image

Thomas F. Cash, *What Do You See When You Look in the Mirror? Helping Yourself to a Positive Body Image* (New York: Bantam, 1995).

Naomi Wolf, *The Beauty Myth: How Images of Beauty Are Used against Women* (New York: Doubleday, 1992).

Psychotherapy

American Psychiatric Association
Code HUP
Division of Public Affairs
1400 K St., N.W.
Washington, DC 20005
Publications: Write for a set of pamphlets about various mental disorders.

American Psychological Association
750 First St., N.E.
Washington, DC 20002-4242
202-336-5500

National Institute of Mental Health
Rm. 7C-02
5600 Fishers Lane
Rockville, MD 20857
301-443-4513

Jack Engler and Daniel Goleman, *The Consumer's Guide to Psychotherapy* (New York: Simon & Schuster, 1992).

Harriet G. Lerner, *Women in Therapy* (New York: Harper & Row, 1988).

Jean Baker Miller, *Toward a New Psychology of Women,* rev. ed. (Boston: Beacon Press, 1986).

Alternative Therapies

OAM Public Information Center
Office of Alternative Medicine
National Institutes of Health
Suite 450
6120 Executive Blvd.
Rockville, MD 20892-9904
301-402-2466
General information packet available by return fax or mail by calling
the main number.

On the Internet: The Alternative Medicine Homepage
(http://www.pitt.edu/~cbw/altm.html), maintained by the Falk Library
of Health Sciences at the University of Pittsburgh, has links to many
other sites on the net. A good commercial online database is AMED
(Allied & Alternative Medicine), compiled by the Medical Information
Centre of the British Library. AMED can be accessed through DataStar
Information Retrieval or Knight-Ridder Information at
http://www.rs.ch/wwv/rs/ds/amed.html.

Joan Borysenko, *Minding the Body, Mending the Mind* (New York: Bantam, 1988).

David Eisenberg, *Encounters with Qi: Exploring Chinese Medicine* (New
York: Viking, 1987).

Bill Moyers, *Healing and the Mind* (New York: Doubleday, 1993).

Index